Dictionary of
COIN NAMES

Also by Adrian Room

Room's Dictionary of Confusibles
Room's Dictionary of Distinguishables
Room's Classical Dictionary
Dictionary of Confusing Words and Meanings
Place-name changes since 1900: A World Gazetteer
Naming Names: A Book of Pseudonyms and Name Changes
  with a 'Who's Who'
Dictionary of Trade Name Origins
Dictionary of Cryptic Crossword Clues
Dictionary of Translated Names and Titles
Dictionary of True Etymologies

Dictionary of

COIN NAMES

Adrian Room

London and New York
Routledge & Kegan Paul

First published in 1987 by
Routledge & Kegan Paul Ltd
11 New Fetter Lane, London EC4P 4EE

Published in the USA by
Routledge & Kegan Paul Inc.
in association with Methuen Inc.
29 West 35th Street, New York, NY 10001

Set in 10 on 12pt Times
by Columns of Reading
and printed in Great Britain
by TJ Press (Padstow) Ltd
Padstow, Cornwall

© *Adrian Room 1987*

Library of Congress Cataloging in Publication Data
Room, Adrian.
  Dictionary of coin names.
  Bibliography: p.
  1. Coins—Names—Dictionaries. I. Title.
CJ69.R66   1987   737.4'03   86-12273

British Library CIP Data also available
ISBN 0–7102–0646–1

CONTENTS

And they brought unto him a penny. And he saith unto them, Whose is this image and superscription? They say unto him, Caesar's.

(Matthew 22: 19–21)

INTRODUCTION

'I took the two precious ornaments that my friend had given me into the large hall, where a great number of people walked slowly along the many racks and doorless cabinets, from time to time choosing, as they proceeded, a gaily coloured article and placing it in a sort of metal net that they carried or that they pushed before them along the ground. By now feeling parched with the unnatural heat, I made my way with some difficulty to a display of pretty crystal vessels containing coloured liquids of different kinds, and after a little hesitation selected one with a delicate picture of a flowery field and with some wording in the native language. Following the example of others, I then joined one of a number of small processions that led to a young woman seated on a sort of tabouret before a curious instrument not unlike the musical one shown me the previous day by my friend in a house of worship nearby. It was, however, much reduced in size and as I drew nearer I observed that its panels were apparently pressed, not pulled. When I finally reached the maid, who was elegantly attired in the green and white robes that her fellow servants also wore, I placed the crystal vessel before her and presented her with the two ornaments, as I had seen others do. She accepted them with no sign of ceremony or gratitude and did not pause to admire their craftsmanship or gaze at the finely executed portrait, as I had spent much time doing. Nor did she even appear to read any part of the inscription, whether on the curved edge of the ornament or on its flat surface. Instead, having depressed two or three of the panels before her, she dropped the fine pieces in a sort of shallow coffer that appeared, selected from it three other ornaments of varying size but noticeably duller hue, and placed them in my hand

1

together with a small piece of script that had somehow been manufactured by the machine. I instantly began to study my new treasures, and endeavoured to make out how they differed from the two beautiful tokens I had now parted with, but a sonorous tone behind me gave me to understand that I was hindering the progress of others in the procession who wished to give the young maiden ornaments of their own. I therefore carefully raised my crystal flask, and holding it firmly in one hand and my new gifts in the other, made my way towards the exterior of the place, where my friend had intimated he would attend me . . .'

This latter-day Swiftian pastiche is designed to serve as a reminder of the basic transactions and procedures involved in making a simple supermarket purchase: the offering of coins as payment and the possible return of coins as change. We very much tend to take the coins themselves for granted, since they are simply a means to an end. Yet for centuries now the transfer of coins in this way for a purchase or a service has been one of the most important features of our daily life and very existence. We get what we need and what we want by giving coins, and by being given them in return for own own work or goods. Even where, as increasingly today, no actual coins change hands, we nevertheless use their names to specify the amount of money involved: we make a cheque out for 6 **pounds** and 50 **pence**, for example, or read in the paper that the pound is now worth 12 French **francs** or 4 **deutschmarks**. (In January 1985, the pound caused consternation by falling so low that it nearly equalled 1 **dollar**.)

All these names are or have been those of coins. What do they mean, though? Why is a pound so called, and a dollar a dollar? Is the French franc named after its native land? What other marks are there beside 'deutsch' ones? And how about all those other coin names, both historic and modern, such as the **doubloon**, the **peseta**, the **rouble**, the **yen**, the **shilling**, the **rupee** and the **anna**? How about the humble **penny**?

Coins are interesting and fascinating objects in their own right, real works of art in many cases, with intriguing depictions and inscriptions. But their names are interesting, too, and in our keenness to study and collect the pieces themselves, or our casualness in using them to do our daily shopping, the names can be so easily overlooked. Even many informative and specialised numismatic works do not explain the meanings of the names. So here now is a new dictionary which aims to explain the names of nearly 1000 coin denominations around the world and which deals, therefore, with a sadly neglected subject: numismonyms (a coined name for coin names!).

It may be helpful for the reader to glance first at the two Appendices at the end of the book, where there are extensive examples, in both categories and 'families', of the types of coin name that exist. It will be seen, if only from the length of some of the lists, that on the whole coins are named after what appears on them (what numismatists call the 'type'), such as a portrait, a value in some currency or other, an inscription, or a device of some kind. For example, I take an old predecimal British penny that I keep as a sentimental souvenir of its day, and examine it. On the obverse (the 'head' side) I see a youthful head and shoulders of Queen Elizabeth II surrounded by a Latin inscription, which runs: ELIZABETH II DEI GRATIA REGINA F: D: ('Elizabeth II by the Grace of God Queen, Defender of the Faith'). Turning it over, on the reverse I find a stylised portrait of a seated and helmeted Britannia (a female personification of Britain), holding a trident in her raised left hand, while her right rests on a large oval shield bearing the British national flag, the 'Union Jack'. Behind her, as she faces right, is the sea, and to the left of her (behind her back) is a lighthouse: Britannia rules the waves! To left and right of the portrait appear respectively two words: ONE PENNY, and below her is the date: 1966. The coin's name appears on it, therefore, but if it didn't (and even conceivably if it did), we might be calling the penny an 'Elizabeth', after the monarch portrayed on the obverse (or from her name there), or a 'Britannia', or even a 'Trident' or a 'Lighthouse'. If the trident had been poorly executed we might now be calling the coin a 'Pitchfork' or a 'Toaster', and if the date had been unusually prominent or significant in some way, the penny might have come to be nicknamed a 'Clicker' (short for 'clickety-click', as the slang term for 'sixty-six' called at bingo). A glance through the Dictionary will show that such apparently fanciful namings are well within the bounds of possibility: see **coquibus**, **dog**, and **horse and jockey**, for example, or (perhaps even better, although not of English origin) **botdrager**.

Most coins over the centuries have borne a portrait (usually of the reigning or ruling monarch under whom it was first issued), a value (denomination), or an inscription, or quite possibly all three, as the penny just described. Rather more original are the different devices that have come to appear on coins since the earliest times, and that have given them their names. Four important ones appear in Appendix II (p.243): the cross, the crown, the lion and the shield. On other coins animals apart from the lion have also featured, as have various birds and flowers. Examples are the lamb on the **agnel**, the **eagle** and the **quetzal** on the coins so named, and the rose on the **rose noble**. Many such devices are already familiar to most people from their use elsewhere as national or religious symbols. Of the four first mentioned here, the cross is one of the oldest, found as a symbol of the Christian church from the 3rd century AD on coins struck in the time of Constantine the Great. This particular device had a practical use, too, since it could carefully divide different parts of an inscription, and even serve as a physical dividing or 'breaking' point when the coin was cut into four quarters, as happened with the medieval English penny (thus making **farthings** or 'fourths'). The crown, of course, is the supreme symbol of the monarchy and of royalty, with different types of crown representing different ranks of ruler (kings, grand dukes, princes, counts, and so on). The lion, long regarded as a symbol of power (the 'king of beasts'), has figured on coins of Ancient Greece and Rome, so has even predated the cross. With the advent of heraldry, it was to become, together with the eagle, one of the most popular heraldic beasts, found on royal coats of arms in many countries of Europe. The shield represents the most common type of defensive weapon of ancient times and the Middle Ages, before the invention of firearms, and like the lion is also found on the early coins of Greece and Rome. Later, the shield became the special heraldic device used for displaying a particular coat of arms. The study of coins thus to a considerable extent overlaps the study of heraldry, since the background and history of the two are complementary. Today, for example, heraldry has itself special names for different types of crosses, crowns, lions and shields, each having its own particular significance.

Appendix II also shows how certain popular coin names have spread and been copied from language to language, sometimes in translated form, but quite often simply as a mere adaptation of a non-native name. See **cent** and **grosso** for some examples of Far Eastern and Arabic renderings, respectively.

Looked at another way, the Dictionary shows that there are really two kinds of coin name – the official and the unofficial. The first of these is usually the actual denomination, used for the value, either consciously chosen to convey a particular meaning, such as a 'royal' name, or borrowed less originally from an existing coin name. (See List 15 in Appendix I, p.241, for several examples.) The second, the unofficial name, is very often simply a popular nickname, arising perhaps as a misidentification of a device on the coin, or given mischievously for some reason. There are plentiful examples of these throughout the book, especially among the many variants on '**thaler**'.

In modern times, alas, coin names have become increasingly functional and prosaic, and nicknames are given less and less frequently. In Britain, for instance, the former **half-crown** has had no successor, the **florin** has become simply the 'ten-p piece', the **shilling** or **bob** has become the 'five-p piece', and both the **sixpence** (or **tanner**) and the **farthing** are now defunct. Nor has any distinctive name been used for the new two-penny coin. Even the penny is often referred to as a 'p' or, as an actual coin in a multiple sum, a 'one-pence piece'. (Many shop assistants will name a total sum of £1.01 as 'one pound, one pence'.)

One might have supposed that some distinctive name would have been used for the novel 50-pence coin, when it was first issued (in 1969), especially in view of its heptagonal shape. The most that could be managed was a half-hearted quip through the media, however, that the piece should be called a 'Wilson', since, like the Prime Minister of the day, Harold Wilson, it was 'many-sided and two-faced'. (With some justification, the coin could actually have been called the 'Britannia', since by popular request the portrait on the old penny was preserved on the new 50-pence piece.)

Three factors make the study of coin names (what might be called 'numismonymics') especially complex.

The first is that most coin names round the world have remained in their native languages, and one thus needs something of an encyclopaedic knowledge of languages to be able to decipher them at all meaningfully. Not only does one have to deal in names in French, Spanish, German, Russian, Arabic, Chinese and Japanese, to quote some of the major languages involved, but one must be able to disentangle similar names, or ones of identical meaning, in different languages, such as the 'cross' names in Appendix II. This is quite a daunting task, and specialist knowledge is needed for some of the more complex languages and scripts (and pronunciations), such as Chinese.

Second, the very course of history has resulted in a bewildering (on the face of it) ramification of coins and currencies, which were formerly not specifically associated with a particular country or state, as they are now, but passed from land to land and hand to hand over a wide territory, especially in Europe. Thus, various kinds of 'pennies' and 'crowns' were imported into England, while many of her own denominations circulated on the other side of the Channel, if only because of the close ties with France before the Hundred Years War (and also the 'Auld Alliance' between France and Scotland, which lasted to the 16th century). A particular type of coin, too, would act as a model for others, which not only resembled it, sometimes quite closely, but were actually named after it, as already mentioned. An even more wide-ranging dispersal of currencies followed with the expansion of various colonial empires, so that British and French coins were current in Africa, for example, Portuguese in the Indian colonies, and also South America, and Spanish currency in both North and South America. The intermingling and mutual adoption of currencies in the Far East, too, adds to the complexity and intricacy of the scene.

Third, many popular and widely circulating coins went by different names, so that the **peso**, for example, was also called the 'Spanish dollar' and a 'piece of eight', the latter familiar from Stevenson's *Treasure Island*. The deceptively simple name 'penny', too, is more complicated than it seems, since the denomination has been used over the centuries to refer to a whole range of coins, from the silver Roman **denarius** (the 'penny' of the Bible) to simply a word for any small coin or value, as in the expressions 'a pretty penny' and 'watch the pennies'.

One of the best-known coins in the world, the **dollar**, illustrates all three factors. At its most basic, the name originates from the German word for 'valley', *Thal* (modern *Tal*), which in this particular case was the generic term that was part of the place name *Joachimsthal* ('St Joachim's valley'), which was in turn used as that of a silver mine in this valley. The output of the mine (or mines, for there were more than one) was so vast that the resulting coin, struck from the local silver, circulated widely in a variety of different types. Hence the reason why 'thaler' features so frequently in the Dictionary with different distinguishing names added, from the **dornenkranztaler** to the **kammerherrentaler**, and from the **Maria Theresa thaler** to the **siebenkopfstücktaler**. Apart from this, the basic name 'thaler' was itself modified as the coin or its copy was introduced in one country after another, until finally it became the American dollar, thousands of miles from the valley in Bohemia that had originally given it its name. Moreover, in North America 'dollar' was the name used for the Spanish peso (hence the alternative name of 'Spanish dollar' for this coin), with the word used in this meaning some two hundred years before the 'proper' American dollar was first issued, in 1794. Nor did the name bypass Britain, since in Scotland in the 16th century the 30-shilling piece was known as a 'sword dollar' and the double **merk** as a 'thistle dollar'. The name became an official denomination, too, a hundred years later, under Charles II, so that this also precedes the American dollar.

Although colloquial names, as mentioned, seem to be less commonly created today, new coin names are nevertheless needed for new currencies, especially when a country switches from an old 'colonial' currency to its

7

own native one, or when it adopts a decimal system. It is therefore not surprising that a number of recent coin names of the 20th century should be found in Africa, just as many of the world's modern place-names are also in that continent. Examples of such names, all entered in the Dictionary, are the **cedi**, **kwacha**, **kwanza**, **leone**, **lilangeni**, **naira**, **ngwee**, **pula**, **syli**, **tambala**, **thebe** and **zaire**. Many of these first appeared in the 1960s or even 1970s.

Mention of colloquial names is not simply coincidental here, since a number of important popular names of coins have their own entries in the Dictionary, thus distinguishing it from most numismatic works, which do not normally consider nicknames, let alone explain them. In fact, such nicknames are much more numerous than might be supposed, and could even fill a dictionary of their own. Many, however, are historic or transient ones, such as the fifty or so listed for the dollar in *The American Thesaurus of Slang*, and will not feature here. Even so, a good proportion are represented, both old and new, and can be found in both English and non-English languages (the latter often as a compound name for the German 'thaler').

The Dictionary even contains some 'ghost' names: names of coins that were planned but never issued, or at most struck only as patterns (prototypes). Among such names are the English **mill** and **victoria**, the Dominican Republic **dominicano** and the Russian **rus**. The coins may never have materialised, but the names are real enough and so deserve to be included here. Almost in the same category, although the coins were actually struck, were the optimistic **spesmilo** and **stelo**, both proposed by the international Esperanto movement. The Common Market **écu** really belongs here, too.

A word should be said about the entries themselves, and what the reader may expect to find there.

The names in the headings are given in their accepted English form, which frequently drops an accent from the foreign original. For non-English names, the accepted plural form is given for the more common names that do not simply add 's', such as *scudi* for **scudo** and *drachmai* for **drachma**. Many African and Oriental names have a plural that is the same as the singular, and this is likewise

8

indicated. Unfortunately, the precise plural form for many coin names is not always fixed in English, and there are often cases where alternatives are possible. For instance, it is not wrong to use 'drachmas' as a plural of **drachma**, since the name has become anglicised to a large extent. Similarly **kwanza** can take an 's' in the plural or remain the same, as can **zloty**. Some coin names, too, have alternative spellings, and this is usually indicated, with a second version given in brackets.

Since most coins are closely linked historically and geographically with the monarch who issued them, a large number of entries contain information about such a monarch, identifying him or her and giving dates as appropriate. In the latter connection it should be noted that a monarch's dates are those of his or her *reign*, not birth and death. Thus Erik XIV, King of Sweden, was born in 1533 and died in 1577 (probably poisoned). He reigned, however, for only nine years, from 1560 to 1568, and these are the dates given to pinpoint the period when he issued the **ferding**.

Where an inscription (usually a Latin one) is quoted, it will normally be translated, and linguistically knowledge-able readers are asked to make allowances for what may appear to be an over-obvious spelling-out of the sense (which may not always be so obvious after all).

Values, too, are given, expressed in multiples or fractions, simply in order to indicate a particular coin's monetary role in its own currency. Changes in the value of a coin over the years (mostly a devaluing) are usually not itemised, unless they are relevant to the name. For full numismatic information about a particular coin, the reader is thus referred to one of the standard reference works included in the Select Bibliography (page 249), or to a historical catalogue. Such details as weight, metal content and so on are not usually given, since they are not normally relevant to the actual name.

Names that are in bold type in an entry refer to a coin name that has its own entry in the appropriate alpha-betical place. The large number of such names is due to the fact that constant cross-referral is often helpful in order to 'place' a coin or its name properly. As already explained, many names are based on those of other coins, for example, as listed in Appendix II.

Finally, it should be stressed that on the whole (although not quite exclusively) the names included in this Dictionary are those of coins 'proper', not those of commemorative tokens, for example, such as the ones issued in modern times to mark the various sports of the Olympic Games. Certainly, some commemorative coin issues are included, such as those of the **thaler**, but these were real coins with a genuine coin name and so deserve to be represented here. It is possible that some of the older denominations may now exist only in the form of banknotes, and at the present time some countries have currencies that consist solely of notes, with a complete absence of coins. (Among them are Paraguay with its **guaranis**, and the Maldive Islands with its **rupees** of a hundred **laris** each.) But these names once applied to coins, so are rightly included. Indeed, they are more 'real' and active today than the 'ghost' denominations included that were never circulated in any form.

A brief Glossary follows this Introduction and explains the more specialised terms that occur in the Dictionary, while at the end of the book, a third Appendix, after the two already mentioned, gives the modern abbreviations and symbols used for many of the world's currencies today. The Select Bibliography then completes the book.

ACKNOWLEDGMENTS

It goes without saying that in a specialist field such as this, advice from experts is not only desirable but even essential, and I should like to record my appreciation of help given by the following in the areas mentioned: Dr Robert Burchfield, Editor of the *Supplement to the Oxford English Dictionary*, for kindly letting me see galley proofs of the relevant coin name entries in Volume IV of the *Supplement* (Se–Z), which was still unpublished at the time this present Dictionary was being completed; Miss B. Burton, Librarian of the School of Oriental and African Studies at the University of London, for obtaining information on coin names of Bhutan; Mr Joe Cribb and Mr Keith Miller, of the Department of Coins and Medals at the British Museum, London, for information on oriental coin names; Mr Iain Orr, of the Foreign and Commonwealth Office, for help with the names of Chinese coins and currencies; Mr J.C. Rapley, of the Universala Esperanto-Asocio (Universal Esperanto Association), Rotterdam, for background information on the **spesmilo** and similarly Mr Geoffrey King, Librarian at the Esperanto Centre, London, for an account of the **stelo**; Mrs Eileen Rees, Customer Relations Officer at the Royal Mint Coin Club, Cardiff, for information on the inscriptions on British **pound** coins; Monsieur B. Schneiter, Conseiller Financier at the French Embassy, London, for information and advice on Mauritanian coin names.

In a more general capacity, but equally valuable, I should like to express my thanks to members of the Book Department of Messrs Spink & Son Ltd, London, who promptly and efficiently kept me up to date with copies of their catalogue (the latest available at the time of writing being *A Catalogue of Numismatic Books*, 1985),

11

and ordered and supplied useful background books as available. A glance through the hundreds of titles of numismatic works listed in their *Catalogue*, itself almost a hundred pages long, shows what a treasure trove of information is available on the subject, from Greek, Roman and Byzantine coins to American and Australian banknotes.

I would also like to thank Messrs Spink & Son Ltd, for providing photographs on pp.23, 47, 57, 72, 79, 102, 103, 104, 112, 119, 121, 149, 158, 179, 183, 197, 201, 214, 223, 224, the Esperanto Society for the photograph of the **stelo** on p.205, the Staatliche Museen, Berlin, German Democratic Republic, for the photograph of the **venustaler** on p.225 and the British Museum for photographs on pp.18, 27, 33, 41, 75, 77, 105, 108, 114, 122, 123, 126, 132, 133, 141, 151, 152, 164, 167, 169, 177, 178, 191, 204, 205, 226, 227, 229 etc.

Adrian Room
Petersfield, Hampshire

GLOSSARY

Anglo-Gallic: a coin struck by an English monarch for his French possessions from the 12th to the 16th centuries, i.e. from Henry II to Henry VIII. Among such coins are the agnel, angelot, blanc, chaise, denier, florin, gros, hardi, leopard, mouton, pavillon and salut.

base (metal): any metal that is not 'precious', i.e. that is not gold, silver or platinum. 'Base' silver is thus silver with an alloy, and a 'base' silver coin is one that should be minted in pure silver but has been **debased** by being minted in such an alloy.

billon: an alloy consisting of gold and silver and some **base metal** such as copper or a coin minted in such an alloy. The word (not to be confused with 'bullion') is Old French for 'ingot'.

clip: to cut a piece from the edge of a coin in order to obtain a small quantity of its precious metal, at the same time reducing its value.

countermark (counterstamp): to punch a mark on a coin for some purpose, usually to change its value or to authorise it for issue in a country other than its original one. Some collectors specialise in countermarked coins.

debase: to reduce the value of a coin by minting it in a metal alloy that has replaced a pure metal, as when a silver coin is reissued in cupro-nickel. Although the *value* of the piece has thus been reduced, it usually bears the same denomination as before. British silver coins such as the shilling and sixpence were thus debased in 1947.

die: the piece of metal that has been engraved (in reverse) with the **obverse** or **reverse** of a coin and that is used to strike or stamp the coin.

incuse: the opposite of 'relief', i.e. concave or hollow, of the design on a coin.

milled coin: strictly, a coin that has been struck by machinery, as distinct from one that has been hammered. Popularly, however, the term is used to mean a coin with a milled edge, one that has a number of serrations, like the former British shilling.

money of account: money that does not exist in actual coinage, but is used for reckoning purposes only, like the guinea until the mid-20th century.

obverse: the 'heads' side of the coin, usually bearing the portrait of the monarch under whom it was issued. Compare **reverse** (below).

radiate: depicted with rays coming from it, as a crown or the sun when borne as a device on a coin.

reverse: the 'tails' side of a coin (compare **obverse**, above). The obverse is regarded as the more important of the two sides, and a reproduction of a coin (such as a photograph or drawing) will usually show the obverse on the left and the reverse on the right.

token: a coin issued unofficially by a trader in former times to be used when there was a shortage of 'proper' coins. In modern times, a 'token' has become a general term for any sort of substitute coin, such as one issued to commemorate some occasion or simply to be used in a slot machine. In a sense, most coins today are in effect 'tokens' since they only represent a fraction of their true value in gold or silver.

type: strictly, the main design on a coin that enables it to be correctly identified. The two most common types are thus the portrait on the **obverse** and the coat of arms on the **reverse** in many cases. Some collectors specialise in collecting as many varieties of a single type as possible. The word can be used in a general sense, however, to mean 'kind', 'sort' (as 'a different type of penny').

abbassi (abassi, abaze)
A base silver Persian coin of the 17th and 18th centuries, named after the shah under whom it was struck, Abbas I (1587–1628). The name was also that of a silver coin of Georgia that circulated subsequently there during the period of independence from Iran. Its value was two Persian abbasi.

abbey crown
A gold **crown** struck in 1526 in the reign of James V of Scotland and named after its place of minting, Holyrood Abbey.

abidi
A half-**rupee** coin of Mysore introduced by the sultan of Mysore, Tipu Sahib (1782–9), in 1786 and named after the fourth Imam, Zainul-abidin (Abid Bimar).

abu midfa
The Arabic name of the Spanish **piastre** in Egypt from the 17th century. It means literally 'father of cannon' and refers to the Pillars of Hercules (representing the Straits of Gibraltar) that were portrayed on the coin but which were taken to be a group of cannon. Similar Arabic names existed for other coins. The **Maria Theresa thaler**, for example, was known as either *abu ṭayr* or *abu kush*, both meaning 'father of a bird' and referring to the double-headed eagle on the reverse, and the Dutch **leeuwendaalder** was known as *abu kalb*, 'father of a dog', applying to the lion on it. Nor were such names (or nicknames) restricted to Egypt. H.L. Rabino's *Coins, Medals and Seals of the Shahs of Iran* (1945) tells how the Dutch **ducat** was known as *bajakli* among the Turkish-

speaking inhabitants of Iran. This literally means 'with legs', and refers to the full-length figure in armour on the obverse. See also **pataca**.

achtbruedertaler
Literally an 'eight-brother-**thaler**'. The name was that of a series of thalers issued in Saxe-Weimar from 1605 to 1619, depicting eight portrait busts of the princes who were the sons of Duke Johann Ernst. Most of the coins had four busts on each side, although one rare version has all eight on the same side.

achtehalber
Literally a 'seven-and-a-halfer', the popular name for the Brandenburg coin current in Prussia in 1720 with a value of one-twelfth of a **thaler** but in 1722 established as worth $7\frac{1}{2}$ Prussian **groschen**. The coin was in circulation in East and West Prussia until 1873.

achtentwintig
A 'twenty-eighter', a silver coin of the Low Countries worth 28 **stuivers** that was first issued in 1601 in Friesland. Other provinces struck the coin, although with a lower silver content, until 1693, when it was withdrawn from circulation.

achtpfenniger
An 'eight-**pfennig**' coin. The name was used for several coins of this value, including the Göttingen körtling of the late 18th century and the **mariengroschen**, as well as various 2-**kreuzer** issues.

achtzehngroscher
An originally Polish coin that was an 'eighteen-**groschen**' piece. It was first minted near the end of the 17th century by the mintmaster Andreas Tympf (see **tympf**) and was the mainstay of Polish currency for over fifty years. The coin was no longer issued after the Seven Years' War (1756–63) when its silver content had become so low as to be unacceptable.

ackey
A silver coin struck in Birmingham, England in 1796 and again in 1818 for use in the Gold Coast (now Ghana). The name was originally that of the weight it represented, this in turn deriving from the seed of the *akee*, a small African tree with edible fruit also known as the 'soapberry'.

adelheidspfennige
A type of medieval German silver **penny**, which, unusually, bore the name of the reigning emperor Otto's consort, Adelheid, on the reverse. The exact reasons for this departure from normal practice are not clear, but it seems likely that Otto attached considerable importance to the lands that Adelheid (or Adelaide) would inherit when he married her in 951.

aes
This is the Latin word for 'bronze' and was the name of the earliest money in Ancient Rome. The original coins were roughcast pieces, now known as *aes rude*. Later, the so-called *aes signatum* appeared as a coin with some kind of design on it. In the second half of the 4th century BC the *aes grave* or 'heavy bronze' coinage was first circulated, being based on the **as** (not to be confused with it) as the unit of value.

affonso de ouro
Literally 'Alfonso of gold', this was the name given to the earliest **cruzado** issued by Alfonso V of Portugal (1438–81).

afghani
This is the principal monetary unit of Afghanistan, divided into 100 **puls**. It was first issued as a silver coin in 1926 in place of the Kabul **rupee**. Today the afghani is a nickel-steel alloy coin.

agnel
A gold coin of France in circulation from the 13th to the 16th centuries. It was so named from the Paschal Lamb that figured on its obverse, with the name itself deriving from Latin *agnellus*, 'little lamb'. It also came to be

19

known in French for the same reason as the **mounton d'or** and must not be confused with the **angel**!

agnus dei

This name has been used of at least two coins. In the 14th century, it was that of a silver coin of Castile issued by John I (1479–90) at Toledo, Burgos and Seville. The name derived from the Latin inscription on it: AGNUS DEI QUI TOLLIS PECCATA MUNDI, part of John 1 : 29 ('the Lamb of God, which taketh away the sin of the world'). Even earlier than this, however, in the late 10th and early 11th centuries, an agnus dei type **penny** was an English one struck by Aethelred II (978–1016) in about the year 1000, apparently to mark the millennium of the Christian era. Unusually, it did not carry the king's portrait on the obverse but a representation of the Lamb of God. The coin is a very rare one.

agora (plural, agorot)

This coin is one-hundredth of the Israeli **pound** (i.e. **shekel**), and in Modern Hebrew has a name that simply means 'small coin' (*ăgōrāh*).

akce

A small silver coin of the Ottoman Empire, introduced as the sole denomination in 1328 under the sultan Urkhan. Its name is Turkish for 'whitish', referring both to its colour and to the fact that it was modelled on the **asper** of Trebizond.

akhtar

A copper 5-**cash** coin of Mysore, introduced by Tipu Sahib in 1792, and given an astronomical name by him, as for other coins of this period. The word is Arabic for 'star'. Compare **bahram**, **kutb**, **mushtari** and **zahrah**.

alberetto (albero)

This was the popular name of the **baiocco**, struck in the Papal States in 1797. It derives from the representation of a Phrygian cap on the coin, which was taken to be a tree (Italian *albero*) or shrub (*alberetto*). The cap is shown on the fasces (bundle of rods with an axe protruding) borne by a lictor (ancient Roman official), and this added to the resemblance to a small tree.

albertin

A gold coin of the Spanish Netherlands, struck in about 1600 after these provinces had been ceded by Philip II of Spain to the Archduke Albert of Austria and his consort Isabella of Spain. The name thus derives from that of the archduke, whose half-length portrait appeared on the coin, together with that of Isabella. See also **albertustaler** (below).

albertustaler

This is the German name for the coin known by the Spanish as a *patagon*. It was a **thaler** of the Netherlands struck in 1612 and named after the Austrian archduke Albert and his consort Isabella who had introduced it, that is, after the same royal couple who had given their name to the **albertin** (above). In German territory the coin was also known as a **kreuzthaler** ('cross thaler'), for the St Andrew's cross on the reverse.

albus

The name is short for Latin *denarius albus*, literally 'white penny' (hence its native German name of *Weisspfennig*). It was a silver coin of the **groschen** type struck in the territory of the Lower Rhine from the second half of the 14th century, and later in other German states. The high silver content of the coin gave it an almost white appearance and hence its name.

alderman

A colloquial name for the **half-crown** in Britain in the 19th century, with a sort of punning reference to the coin as a kind of 'half-king', since the alderman was the chief magistrate in his ward or district and in Algo-Saxon times had actually been a deputy (viceroy) for the king. Strangely, the sense is not recorded in the *Oxford English Dictionary*.

alfonsino

The name of various coins referring to a ruler called Alfonso. Among them were a silver **denier** of Alfonso IV of Portugal (1325–57) and a new type of **gigliato** named after Alfonso V of Aragon as king of Sicily (1416–58) and Naples (1443–58). The gold **ducatone** of this same king was also popularly known as an *alfonsino d'oro*, or 'gold alfonsino'.

alicorno

A silver coin of Ferrara, issued by Duke Hercules I (1471–1505) at a value of 12 **quattrini**. It was named after the figure of a unicorn on the reverse (modern Italian *unicorno* or *liocorno*).

aloëtaler

The popular name of a **thaler** issued in Germany in 1701 to commemorate the first blossoming of an aloe tree introduced to the country a few years previously.

altilik

A Turkish coin of base silver issued from 1833 to 1839 at a value of 6 **piastres**. The name derives from the Turkish word for 'six', *altı*. Compare **altmishlik** and **artilucco** (below).

altmishlik

A silver coin of the Ottoman Empire equal to 1½ **piastres** or 60 **paras**. Its name refers to the latter, since it derives from the Turkish for 'sixty', *altmış*. Compare **altilik** (above) and see also **utuzlik**.

altun

A Turkish gold coin first issued in 1454 to replace the Venetian **ducat** or **zecchino**. The latter name led to the coin also being known as a **sequin**. Its Turkish name comes from the word for 'gold', *altın*. Compare **altyn** (below).

altyn

A small Russian coin of the 14th century, at first equal to 6 Moscow **dengi** and later to 3 Novgorod dengi. (The latter value led to the emergence of the **novgorodka** and **kopeck**.) In 1654 a copper coin known as the *altynnik* appeared, and from 1704 to 1726 a silver altyn was in circulation. The name, however, is simply the Tatar word for 'gold' (compare **altun**, above). Although now a coin of the past, the modern 15-kopeck piece in Russia is still known colloquially by some older people as *pyatialtynny*, 'five-altyn coin', after the value of the Novgorod piece.

amani
A gold coin of Afghanistan, introduced in 1926 by the ruler after whom it is named, Amānollāh Khān (1919–29). It had a value of 20 **afghani**, but was not issued after 1936.

ambrosino
The name of a gold or silver coin of Milan in circulation from 1250 to 1310 and continued by the ruling dynasty, the Sforzas, to the end of the 15th century. The coin received its name from St Ambrose, the patron saint of Milan, whose portrait appeared on the obverse (usually standing, but occasionally on horseback).

amedeo d'oro
A 'golden Amadeus', the name of a gold coin of value 10 **scudi** issued under the rule of Victor Amadeus I, Duke of Savoy (1630–7), whose Italian name of Vittorio Amedeo is more accurately reflected in that of the coin. The Duke's portrait appeared on the obverse.

anconitano (agontano)
A variation of the **grosso** struck at Ancona in the 13th century and taking its name from the Italian city. The value of the coin was set at 12 **denarii**.

ange d'or
A 'golden angel', a large French gold coin, first struck by Philip VI of Valois (1328–50) and bearing a picture of the Archangel Michael (see **angel** and **angelet**).

angel
An English gold coin, originally called an 'angel noble' (after its value, of one **noble**, or 6 **shillings** and 8 **pence**), and introduced by Edward IV in 1465. Its obverse showed the Archangel Michael spearing the Dragon, a device based on that of the **ange d'or**. The coin was a popular one from the time of Henry VIII to that of Elizabeth I, but it was no longer minted after 1634, during the reign of Charles I.

angelet
A 'little angel', or a gold coin value half an **angel** and first issued in the same year as its 'big brother'. Its life was

not so long, however, and it was discontinued in 1619, in the reign of James I. Its device of the Archangel Michael defeating the Dragon was based, like that of the angel itself, on the French **ange d'or**.

angelot

Like the English **angelet**, a 'little angel'. The coin was an Anglo-Gallic one, first issued in the early 15th century and valued at two-thirds of the **salut**. The obverse showed a figure of an angel holding a cross and shield, together with the arms of England and France.

angster

A silver coin of Switzerland, in circulation from the mid-14th to the mid-19th century, by which time it had been debased to a copper coin. According to some authorities, its name derives from German *Angesicht*, 'face', with reference to the portrait of the Bishop of Basel on one side. It is much more likely, however, that the word developed from Medieval Latin *angustus*, 'thin', since the original coin was a one-sided **bracteate**.

ang tuk

A silver coin struck in Nepal in 1696 for circulation in Tibet. The Nepali name has the meaning 'number six', referring to the last figure in the date of 816, the year when it was first minted according to the calendar of the Newar, the people of mixed descent who inhabit Nepal.

anna

An Indian copper coin with a value of one-sixteenth of a **rupee**. It first circulated in the 18th century and was in use until the introduction of decimal currency in 1957 (in Pakistan, 1961), when the rupee was divided into 100 new **paise** instead. The Hindi name of the coin, *āṇā*, ultimately derives from a Sanskrit word, meaning 'small'.

annunciata

The colloquial name of a coin issued by the Italian princely family of Gonzaga in Guastalla in the 16th century. The coin, with a value of 14 **soldi**, had a representation of the Annunciation on the obverse, hence the name.

anselmino
The name of a double **giulio** issued in Mantua, Italy, by Prince Vicenzo Gonzaga (1587–1612). This silver coin, with a value of 20 **soldi**, had a portrait of St Anselm of Lucca, patron saint of Mantua, on the obverse.

annengroschen
The name given to the **groschen** bearing a portrait of St Anne (mother of the Virgin Mary) that was struck in the first half of the 16th century in a number of towns in Lower Saxony. The silver coin was worth one-twelfth of a Rhine **goldgulden**.

antoninianus
A silver Roman coin that was named after the emperor who introduced it in AD 215. This was Marcus Aurelius Antoninus, usually better known by his nickname of Caracalla (from the type of long hooded tunic that he also introduced). The coin gradually replaced the **denarius** as the main silver coin, although by the mid-3rd century it had already been debased to little more than a copper piece. The antoninianus bore a portrait of the emperor, with however a radiate crown and not a laurel wreath, as on most other Roman coins. It had a value as a double denarius.

aparas
A Portuguese silver coin struck for circulation in the country's Indian possessions. The name derives from Portuguese *aparar*, 'to trim', 'clip', so that the coin was actually cut from the **piastre** and then counterstamped.

apollina
A colloquial name in Sicily for the gold coins of Syracuse that were issued in the 4th century BC in the reign of Agathocles. The obverse bore a head of Apollo.

apuliensis
The name of a silver coin of the **denarius** type struck in the late 12th century in Palermo and Salerno by William II of Sicily. The name is Latin for 'of Apulia', referring to the region of south-east Italy. Palermo is in Sicily and Salerno in Campania, but the coin was also issued in

Brindisi, Apulia, by the emperor Henry VI in 1195, so that it was fully called the *denarius apuliensis*.

ardit
A small copper coin of Barcelona struck by Philip III (1598–1621) and in circulation to the mid-18th century. The name is said to derive from the two letters A and R that stood on either side of the king's portrait on the original types and which stood for *Aragoniae Rex*, 'king of Aragon'.

arendrijksdaalder
Literally, the 'eagle state **thaler**', from Dutch *arend*, 'eagle' and *rijk*, 'state'. This was the name of a thaler issued in the Netherlands (originally in Friesland) in the late 16th century and which bore on the reverse a representation of an eagle as a symbol of state. Later issues of the coin had the eagle on the obverse. Compare **arendschelling** and **arendsdaalder** (below).

arendschelling
An 'eagle **shilling**', the silver coin introduced in the Netherlands in 1536 by the emperor Charles V. The piece had a value of 4 **stuivers** (6 from 1586) and bore an imperial eagle on the reverse. It was also known as an **escalin**.

arendsdaalder
An 'eagle **thaler**' issued in the Netherlands provinces of Zeeland and Friesland, respectively in 1601 and 1617. The obverse bore the imperial eagle, and the reverse a shield. Compare **arendrijksdaalder** (above).

argenteus
A Roman silver coin equal to a **denarius** that was struck until the time of Julian (361–3). The name is simply Latin for 'of silver', 'made of silver'.

argentino
A gold coin of the Argentine first issued in 1881 at a value of 5 **pesos**. The name is that of the country (whose own name, however, means 'silver'!).

armelino (armellino)
A silver coin of Italy, valued at half a **carlino** and issued by Ferdinand I, king of Naples (1458–94). The name comes from the representation of an ermine (modern Italian *ermellino*). The animal was popularly taken to be a fox, however, which led to the coin also acquiring the name *volpetta* ('little fox').

artilucco (artiluk)
A silver coin of the republic of Ragusa current from 1627 to 1701 and having a value of 3 **grossetti**. It was based on the Polish 3-**groschen** piece (the **trojak**), and, since this itself was valued at 6 **paras**, the artilucco acquired a name derived from Turkish *altiluk*, meaning 'sixfold' (see **altilik**).

as (plural, asses)
The word is the Latin for 'unit', and originally the name, like English **pound**, was that of a unit of weight. This then transferred to the equivalent weight of metal, then to the coin which represented the value of such metal. (Originally, it was divided into 12 ounces or **unciae**, and the weight was judged to be what could be reasonably supported on the hand of an outstretched arm.) First issued in about 200 BC, the coin gradually reduced in size, weight and value, so that by the time of Augustus (27 BC–AD 14) it roughly approximated to the English pre-decimal **halfpenny**. The entire Roman monetary system was based on the as (see **aes**).

ashrafi
A Persian gold coin in circulation from the 15th to the 18th centuries, when it was superseded by the **toman**. The name comes from Arabic *ashrāf*, plural of *sharīf*, 'noble', referring to the noble lineage and preeminence in Islam of the Sufi dynasty who issued it. See also **seraph**.

asmani (usmani)
A copper 40-**cash** coin of Mysore, issued by Tipu Sahib in 1789 and named after the third caliph (*khalīfa*) 'Usman-ibn-'Affan. See also **mushtari**.

asper

A small base silver coin current in the Middle East from the 13th to the 15th centuries and corresponding to the European **denier** of the time. Its name derives through French *aspre* or Italian *aspero* from Byzantine Greek *aspron*, referring to its colour. The Turkish **akce** was based on it.

atchison (acheson)

A copper coin coated with silver that was struck in the reign of James VI of Scotland (James I of Great Britain), equal to 8 Scottish **pennies** or two-thirds of an English penny. The name represents the Scottish pronunciation of the surname Atkinson, which was that of the Edinburgh mintmaster at the beginning of James VI's reign.

aubonne

A name for a variety of **écu** struck for the French duchy of Lorraine and Bar (Barrois) in the 18th century by monsieur d'Aubonne, director of the mint for the four years from 1724.

augustalis

A gold coin struck in the reign of Emperor Frederick II when king of Sicily as Frederick I (1198–1250) and issued in Messina and Brindisi. It was based on the ancient Roman **aureus** and derived its name from its imperial inscription: FRIDERICUS IMPERATOR ROMAN-ORUM CAESAR AUGUSTUS. Italian numismatists refer to the coin by the name of *agostaro*.

august d'or

A gold coin struck in the 1750s by Frederick Augustus II, Elector of Saxony (1733–63), otherwise Augustus III, king of Poland. The piece was based on the **friedrich d'or**, which itself was a copy of the **louis d'or**. The august d'or had a value of 5 **thalers**, and this was indicated on the coin, which was also current from 1777 to 1845.

aurar

The plural of **eyrir** (which see).

aureus

This was the standard gold coin of Ancient Rome, with a value of 25 **denarii** or 100 **sestertii**. It was introduced by Caesar in about 49 BC. Its name means simply 'golden' (i.e. implying *denarius aureus*), but like other Roman coins it gradually decreased in weight and value until in the time of Constantine (306–37) it was superseded by the **solidus**.

austral

A currency introduced in Argentina in June 1985 to combat inflation, with a value of 1000 **pesos**. Its name is Spanish for 'southern', referring to the location of Argentina in South America.

azzalino

A version of the **testone** issued by the Paleologi (the last dynasty of Byzantine emperors) in the 14th century. The name is a corruption of Italian *acciarino*, 'steel for striking fire', from a representation of this on the coin. Compare **briquet.**

B

bagattino (bagateno)
Originally a colloquial name for the silver **denaro** (the so-called *denaro piccolo*, or 'little denaro') of northern Italy. The name, which means 'small change' (compare English 'bagatelle'), is first recorded in documents dated 1274 in Padua. Later, the name was adopted for a copper coin struck in Reggio in 1477 and circulating in various types and weights until 1573.

bahram (behram)
A copper 5-**cash** piece of Mysore introduced by Tipu Sahib, Sultan of Mysore, in 1790 and with a name deriving from the Persian word for the planet Mars.

baht (bat)
The basic monetary unit of Thailand, equal to 100 **satang**. It was introduced in 1928 to replace the **tical**, but has not entirely ousted this earlier name for the coin. Its name represents Thai *bāt*, 'quarter', since it was originally regarded as a quarter of a **tael**, the standard silver weight of eastern Asia.

baiocco (plural, baiocchi)
A coin of the Papal States with a value of one-hundredth of a **scudo**. Originally, in the 15th century, it was struck in base silver. Later, from 1720, it was a copper denomination, and was struck in vast quantities from 1800 to 1866. Its name refers to its colour, deriving from Italian *baio*, 'bay-coloured'.

baiza
A copper coin of Somalia when it was an Italian colony (as Italian Somaliland), first issued in 1909. Its name

derives from colloquial Arabic and is the same in origin as that of the **paisa**. Today the baiza is one-thousandth of a **rial** in Oman.

bakiri (bakhri)

A coin with a value of a quarter of a **rupee** of Mysore, introduced in 1786 by the Sultan of Mysore, Tipu Sahib. Its name pays tribute to the fifth Imam, Muhammad Bakir.

balboa

A coin of Panama worth 100 **centesimos**, and named after Vasco Nuñez de Balboa, the Spanish explorer who discovered the Pacific in 1513.

ban (plural, bani)

The Romanian copper coin, 100 of which make a **leu**, was first issued in 1867. Its name ultimately derives from Persian *bān*, 'lord': compare other 'title' names such as **augustalis** and **bargellino** (below).

banderuola

A colloquial name for the **ducatone** struck in Italy by Odoardo Farnese, fifth duke of Parma and Placentia (Piacenza) (1622–46), and named after the figure of St Anthony holding a banner (*banderuola*) on the reverse.

barbarin

A base silver coin of the abbey of Saint-Martial, Brittany, issued at the beginning of the 12th century. The name derives from the bearded face of the saint on the obverse (French *barbe*, 'beard'). Compare **barbone** (below).

barbarina

A silver coin of Mantua with a value of 10 **soldi**, depicting the figure of St Barbara, the patron saint of the city.

barberine

A general name for the 5-**soldi** coin struck at Avignon in 1637 by Pope Urban VIII, whose family name was Barberini.

barbone

A silver coin of the Italian republic of Lucca, in circulation from the second half of the 15th century to the mid-18th. The word is Italian for 'man with a long beard', and refers to the bearded face of Christ depicted on the obverse. Compare **barbarin** (above).

bar cent

A copper trial **cent** piece, planned to be struck in about 1776 in the United States as a unit of decimal coinage. The name refers to the 13 lateral bars on one side of the coin, these representing the total number of American states at the time.

bargellino

A coin of 6 **denarii** in value, issued in 1316 by Lando di Agubbio, sheriff (*bargello*) of Florence, and named after his title.

barile

A silver coin of Florence, struck in the early 16th century, and originally having a value of 12 **sols**, 6 **deniers**, an amount that apparently represented the duty or tax on a barrel (Italian, *barile*) of wine.

bastiao

A colloquial name for the silver **xeraphim** struck for the Portuguese possession of Goa in 1659, with a value of 300 **reis** or 5 **tangas**. The name relates to the figure of St Sebastian on the obverse (Portuguese *Bastião*, 'Sebastian').

bat see **baht**.

battezone

A broad silver **grosso** of Florence, issued in the early 16th century. It resembled the **carlino**, and the obverse had a representation of the baptism of Christ by St John. Hence the name, from Italian *battezzare*, 'to baptise'.

batz (batzen)

A silver coin of Switzerland resembling the **groschen** and having a value of 4 **kreuzer**. It was issued in the 15th century, and has a name that is believed to derive from

Old German *bätz* or *betz*, 'bear', referring to the bear
that appeared in the coat of arms of the city of Berne,
where the coin was first minted. Batzen were still in
circulation in the 19th century, at a value of 10 to 1 franc.
See also **rollbatzen**.

bauerngroschen

Literally, 'peasant **groschen**', the colloquial name of the
silver groschen that was struck in the German town of
Goslar in 1477. The name relates to the depiction on the
reverse of the two apostles Simon and Jude carrying a
staff and a saw, implements of the rural farmhand.

bauschen (buschen)

The name of coins of value 12 or 4 **hellers**, struck in the
late 16th century in the imperial German city of Aachen
(Aix-la-Chapelle). The reverse of the coins had a single
or double letter 'B', which may have stood for German
Brot, 'bread', in the manner of token pieces for the poor.
The name does not relate to this, however, but to the
small bunch of flowers that appeared under the value,
from German *Blütenbüschel*, 'bunch of flowers'.

bawbee

A base silver coin of Scotland first struck in 1542 at a
value of 3 Scottish **pennies** (later, 6, or equivalent to the
English **halfpenny**). Attempts have been made to derive
the name from French *basse pièce*, 'base coin' or *bas
bullon*, 'base bullion' (i.e. mixed metal). There has also
been an account explaining the name as a form of 'baby',
from the head of the monarch on it. But the bawbee was
struck near the end of the reign of James VI and in fact
bore no head at all, let alone a baby's. The most likely
origin is in the name of the mintmaster of the time,
Alexander Orok, Laird of Sillebawbee. Other instances
of mintmasters' names or titles in use as coin designations
are known, such as the **atchison** and, very likely, the
bodle (see below).

beato amedeo

A colloquial name for the silver coin, value 9 **fiorini**,
struck in Turin and Vercelli, Italy, by the Duke of Savoy,
Charles Emmanuel I, in 1616. The words are Italian for

'Blessed Amadeus', and refer to the portrait of St Amadeus on the coin.

beichttaler
The name means 'confession **thaler**', and was that of a series of thalers, in particular 1½- and 2-thaler coins, struck in the 17th century by John George (Johann Georg) II, Elector of Saxony. 'Confession' money (there were also 'confession' **groschen** and **pfennigs**) was money handed to a priest by a parishioner after making his confession. The custom was at first voluntary, then compulsory, and was finally abolished.

belga
The name of a banknote value 5 Belgian **francs** issued in Belgium in 1926 and in circulation until the beginning of the Second World War. The reference is not so much to Belgium as to Latin *Belga*, 'member of the Belgae', the race after whom modern Belgium is named.

bender
A colloquial English name current in the 19th century for the **sixpence**, and probably referring to the fact that the coin could be easily bent (compare **crookie**). The name occurs in the works of Dickens and Thackeray, and in *Pickwick Papers*, for example, comes in the following exchange: ' "Will you take three bob?" "And a bender," suggested the clerical gentleman.'

benediktenpfennig
A 'benediction **pfennig**', or a type of pilgrimage pfennig struck in Germany in large quantities from the 17th century. The coin bore a portrait of St Benedict of Nursia, the 5th-century founder of monasticism in western Europe, with, on the reverse, an abbreviated version of St Benedict's blessing, in the form of the letters: 'V.R.S.N.S.M.V.S.M.Q.L.I.V.B.' arranged in a circle. These stood for Latin: 'Vade retro Satana, nunquam suade mihi vana: sunt mala quae libas, ipse venena bibas!', representing a formula against the Devil. The blessing translates as: 'Go away from me, Satan, and do not tempt me with vain things! The wines you offer are bad; may you drink the poisons yourself!' The name

of the coin refers thus both directly to St Benedict and indirectly to his benediction.

ber

A former silver coin of Ethiopia, with the name an alternative for the **talari**. The word is Amharic and basically means 'silver', 'silver coin'. It appeared on the coin in the value: 'Amd Ber' ('one ber'), and is represented today by the **birr**.

berner (perner)

As originally struck, a scyphate (concave) **pfennig** of the 11th century, minted in Verona as a *denarius veronensis*. Its name derives from the Old German name of Verona, *Bern*. Despite its decreasing weight and value, the berner later became the basis for the Austrian **zwanziger**, which was worth 20 berner. It ceased to be in use from about the mid-15th century.

bernhardsgroschen

A silver coin of Hildesheim first current at the end of the 15th century. It is named after St Bernward whose half-length figure appeared on the reverse together with the inscription SAC BERWARDV P. (the latter letter said to stand for Latin *patronus*). St Bernward (not to be confused with St Bernard) was bishop of Hildesheim in the 11th century and is the patron saint of the German city.

besa (plural, bese)

A bronze coin issued from 1909 to 1921 for use in Italian Somaliland, where it had a value of one-hundredth of a **rupee**. The name was also that of a copper coin formerly circulating in Ethiopia, as one-hundredth of a **talari**. In both cases the word is simply an italianised form of **paisa**.

bettlertaler

A **thaler** minted in Schwarzburg, Mainz, Schwyz and Lucca bearing a portrait of St Martin and the beggar on the reverse. German *Bettler* means 'beggar'. It is possible that the coin was based on the **dicken** struck in Colmar in 1499.

bezant (besant)

A gold coin of Constantinople that was the principal gold coin of Europe, including England, from the 4th to the 5th centuries and that was a late form of the **solidus**. The name is a form of Latin *byzantius nummus*, 'Byzantian coin'. In England it was superseded by the **noble**.

bezenstuiver

A colloquial name for the 18th-century **stuiver** of the Netherlands, meaning literally 'broom stuiver'. The reference is to the bundle of arrows shown on the obverse, which resembles a broom or besom.

bezzo

A small Venetian coin introduced in the 16th century during the period of Doge Andrea Gritti. The name is said to derive from Illyrian *becs*, 'small coin'.

biche

An 18th-century French coin minted at Mahé, south-west India, and equal to a **pice**, of which word the name is a corruption. (See **paisa** for the original.)

bigatus

A colloquial name for the Roman **denarius** that on the reverse showed a chariot drawn by two horses, with the Latin word for this vehicle being *biga*.

birr see **ber**.

bissolo

A base silver coin of the duchy of Milan issued in the early 15th century in the time of Giovanni Maria Visconti, and having a value of one-eighteenth of a **soldo**. The reverse bore the arms of the Visconti family, which included a crowned grass snake (Italian *biscia*). Compare **bissona** (below).

bissona

A silver coin struck by Louis XII of France in the early 16th century and having a value of 3 **soldi**. The obverse bore the arms of France between two crowned grass snakes (Italian *biscia*). Compare **bissolo** (above).

bit

A colloquial term for various coins, such as the English threepenny bit, but in particular for the so-called 'cut' coin, that is, one that has had a piece ('bit') cut off the edge or punched from the centre. The best known such coins were originally the Spanish **pieces of eight**, which circulated in the West Indies until the early 19th century, having a value of 1 **real**. In the United States, 'bit' is used as a monetary unit worth one-eighth of a **dollar** (i.e. $12\frac{1}{2}$ **cents**). As such, it is used only in even multiples, e.g. '4 bits', '6 bits', etc.

blaffert (plappart)

A broad silver **bracteate** coin of North Germany current from the 14th to the 16th centuries and originally having a value of 2 **pfennigs**. The name is believed to derive from Dutch *blaf*, 'broad'. However, there were other coins of the name, such as the Swiss and South German blaffert of the 14th century. These were not broad pieces, and their name may therefore derive instead from French *blafard*, 'pale'. The alternative name plappart (or plappert) is simply a German variant of 'blaffert' (also spelt 'blaffart').

blamüser (blaumüser)

A colloquial name for the half-**stuiver** coin struck in Nijmegen, Netherlands, in 1527. Dutch *blau*, literally 'blue', has the association of something of poor or low quality, hence the word came to be used of this poor quality coin, with the name understood in German as *Blaue Mäuse*, 'blue mice', later corrupted to *Blaumüser* or *Blamüser*. In the 16th century the name came to be used of the German *Adlerschilling* ('eagle shilling'), which was a 4-stuiver piece. In the 17th century, this blamüser was minted in large quantities in western Germany when it acquired the name of *Achteltaler*, i.e. 'one-eighth of a **thaler**'.

blanc

French 'white', and the general term for a number of coins that were visibly of pure silver, at least when first struck. The name particularly applies to the French silver coin of the **groschen** type minted in the 14th century, and was also used of the Anglo-Gallic coin copied from it, struck in the reign of Henry VI (1422–61). Compare **blanca** (below) and also **albus**.

blanca
The smallest Spanish billon coin, worth half a **maravedi** and struck from the end of the 15th century. The name of the coin is the Spanish for 'white', referring to the white shining metal of the piece. Compare **blanc** (above) and also **albus**.

blesensis (blesianis)
A general name for French **deniers** struck by the counts of Blois, with the first being the 10th-century ones of Count Thibaut I, founder of the house of Blois-Champagne. The coin bore the head of a wolf, with the Celtic name of this animal (*blez*) being connected with that of Blois itself. This link is false, however, since the place-name is actually pre-Celtic in origin. The coin name, nevertheless, accurately represents the Roman adjectival name of Blois, *Blesensis*.

blob
A copper 5-**cent** coin in circulation in Ceylon (now Sri Lanka) from 1870. The coin was square in shape, and minted from a brass and nickel alloy. The colloquial name is the standard word 'blob' applied to a coin that resembled a small chunk or mass of metal.

bob
A colloquial name for the English **shilling**, in use at least from the 18th century. The origin of the term has been disputed, although it appears to derive from a longer word 'bobstick', where 'bob' meant something small and 'stick' suggests the standard German word for 'coin', *Stück*. It is just possible, however, that the origin lies in the name of Sir Robert Walpole, who was Chancellor of the Exchequer in the 1720s, even though the coin itself is obviously much older than this. The name was still current for a while for the five-**penny** piece even after decimalisation in 1971.

bockstaler
The colloquial name of a **thaler** circulating in the Swiss city and canton of Schaffhausen, bearing a coat of arms showing a ram (German *Bock*) leaping through the city gates.

bodle
A small copper coin of Scotland struck by Charles II (1660–85) for that country and having a value of 2 Scottish **pennies** or one-sixth of an English penny. It is possible that the name represents the surname Bothwell, that of a mintmaster of the time, although there is no documentary evidence for this. The coin was also known as a **turner**.

böhmen
The colloquial name used by the Silesians for the **groschen** of Prague, and probably deriving from the figure of the lion of Bohemia on the coin, as well as the Latin inscription DEI GRATIA REX BOEMIE on it. *Böhmen* is in any case the standard German word for 'Bohemia'.

bolivar (plural, **bolivares**)
A gold coin of Venezuela, named after Simón Bolívar (1783–1830), the South American revolutionary leader who drove the Spaniards from Venezuela, Colombia, Ecuador and Peru, and after whom Bolivia is named. The bolivar was introduced as a monetary unit in 1871, and gold coins of 10, 20, 25, 50 and 100 bolivares were struck, with silver coins of 5, 2, 1 and fractional amounts. The 20-bolivar piece bore a portrait of Bolívar on the obverse. Today the bolivar is the standard unit of the country, divided into 100 **centimos**. Compare **boliviano** (below).

boliviano
From 1864 to 1963, the standard monetary unit of Bolivia, named after Simón Bolívar (see **bolivar**, above). It was divided into 100 **centavos**, but was replaced in 1963 by the **peso**.

bolognino

A silver coin struck in the Italian town of Bologna in the 12th century. It was a type of **denaro**, the so called *bolognino piccolo*, with a value of one-twelfth of a **soldo**. From 1236 the *bolognino grosso* was in circulation, with a value of 12 *bolognini piccoli*. Some popes also issued the coin, and in 1783 a copper bolognino was struck which actually bore its value as *un bolognino*, although the name was originally a colloquial one for the denaro.

bonk

A colloquial name for the copper bar money (rectangular coins) circulating in the Dutch East Indies in the 18th and early part of the 19th centuries. The coins had values ranging from half a **stuiver** to 8 stuivers, and the name is the Dutch word for 'lump', 'mass' (literally 'bone'), with reference to the 'chunky' appearance of the pieces.

bonnet piece

A gold coin of Scotland, first issued under James V in 1539 and having a value of 40 Scottish **shillings**. The coins bore on the obverse a portrait of the king wearing a broad flat cap or 'bonnet', hence the name. The bonnet piece was the first Scottish coin to be dated.

boratinka

The name given to Polish and Lithuanian **shillings (solidi)** struck from 1659 to 1666 by the Polish mintwarden Titus Livius Boratini and named after him.

botdrager

The colloquial name of the 1- and 2-**groot** coins in circulation in Brabant and Flanders in the 14th and 15th centuries. The name is Dutch for 'pot carrier', referring to the lion on the obverse wearing a helmet that resembles an upturned pot.

botinat

A silver coin of Georgia current in the 13th century and so named as it closely resembled the Roman coins struck for the Byzantine Empire in the 11th century by the emperor Nicephorus Botiniates.

brabant

A base silver coin circulating in England at the end of the 13th century and named after its probable place of origin, the Netherlands duchy of Brabant. It had a value of half a **penny**, but was prohibited in 1310.

bracteate

A general term for the thin silver or gold leaf coins found widely in central Europe in the 12th and 13th centuries and stamped on one side only (so that the design appears in mirror image on the reverse). The word derives from Latin *bractea*, 'thin plate of metal'. Such coins originated in Thuringia, so were of Germanic provenance.

bragone

A colloquial name among Italians for the Hungarian **ducat**, struck in the 16th century and circulating widely on foreign markets. The name is a corruption of Italian *brache*, 'breeches', referring to the wide and baggy breeches worn by the figure of the ruler on the coin.

brasher doubloon

A gold coin struck in New York in 1787 and named after its originator, the goldsmith Ephraim Brasher. He had intended to strike copper coins, but since permission was not granted for this he minted gold coins instead.

braspenning

A colloquial and semi-derisory name for the quarter-**stuiver** of Brabant and Flanders, current in the 15th and 16th centuries. It is based on Dutch *bras*, 'worthless thing' (compare German *Braβ*, 'rubbish' and possibly English 'brash').

bremsentaler

The colloquial name for the **thaler** struck in Lübeck, Germany, in 1537, and deriving from the fly (German *Bremse*) appearing on the obverse in the arms of the city's burgomaster, Nicholas von Brömbsen (to act as a visual pun on his name, in the traditional manner of so called 'canting arms').

brillen dukat
The nickname of a gold type of **ducat** of Denmark struck by Christian IV in 1647. The reverse has a pair of spectacles (German *Brille*) together with the Latin inscription: VIDE MIRA: DOMI:, and abbreviated form of VIDE MIRACULA DOMINI, 'See the wonders of the Lord'.

briquet
The French name for the Dutch **vuurijzer**, which depicted a flint and steel (*briquet*). Compare **azzalino**.

broad (broad piece)
Another name for certain coins that were larger and thinner than the standard milled ones. The best known were the **unite**, the gold coin originally worth 20 **shillings** that was struck by James I in 1604, and the hammered 20-shilling piece of Charles II (1660–85), so called to be distinguished from the newly current **guinea** which had the same value. This latter broad was withdrawn in 1732 since it had become considerably diminished in size and value through constant wear and clipping. The James I coin was also known as the **jacobus**.

brown
A colloquial English word for a copper coin in the 19th century, especially a **halfpenny**. There may be some circles where the expression is still in use today, despite the general lack of inventiveness over original names for decimal coins.

brummer
A colloquial German name for Polish $1\frac{1}{2}$-**groschen** coins (**poltoraki**) struck at the beginning of the 17th century in Bydgoszcz. The German name for this city was Bromberg, and it was from this that the coin name derived.

bu
A Japanese coin or unit of currency introduced in 1599 and having a value of a quarter of a **ryo**, or 4 **shu**. The word simply means 'division', 'part'. See **ichebu** as the coin worth 1 bu.

buck

The colloquial American word for a **dollar**. The origin is uncertain, but it is possible the word is short for 'buckskin', referring to the use of deerskins as a unit of exchange when trading with American Indians in early colonisation days. Buckskins were generally held to be more valuable than doeskins.

bugeslawer

A colloquial name for the silver coins struck under Bogislav X (1471–1523), Duke of Pomerania, deriving as a corruption of his name. Unlike other coins of his reign, which merely bore his title (as DUX POMERANIAE), the large silver ones were inscribed with his name.

bungtown

A nickname for a poor imitation of the English **halfpenny** that circulated in the second half of the 18th century in the north-eastern states of America, especially Pennsylvania. The name is based on the slang use of 'bung' to mean 'cheat'.

bun penny

The popular name of the English bronze **penny** struck from 1860 to 1894, showing a young head of Queen Victoria with her hair arranged in a 'bun'.

C

cagnolo

A colloquial name for the billon coin issued in Mantua by Giovanni Francesco Gonzaga in the 15th century. The obverse of the coin portrayed a dog (Italian *cagna*).

caixa (caxa)

A copper coin formerly in circulation in the Malay Peninsula. The word is Portuguese in origin (and happens to mean 'box', 'chest' in that language), so thus derives from the same source (ultimately Latin) that gave English 'cash' (i.e. money).

camillino

The name of a silver coin of Correggio, Italy, bearing on the obverse a bust of the Count of Correggio, Camillo of Austria (1597–1606). The coin had a value of 2 **soldi**.

canary

A former colloquial term in English for the **guinea**, from the yellow colour of the coin. The word was current in the 18th and 19th centuries, and in the latter was also used of a **sovereign**. A similar slang name for both coins was 'yellow boy'.

candareen

A Chinese unit of weight and currency equal to one-hundredth of a **tael**. The word derives from Malay *kěnděri* which itself comes from Tamil *kunri*, the name of the Indian licorice plant (*Abrus precatorius*) whose berries were originally used as weights.

capellone

A colloquial Italian name for a silver coin worth one-third of a **lira** struck in Modena in the 18th century by Francesco III d'Este. The name, Italian for 'long-haired person', refers to this feature on the portrait appearing on the coin.

carantano (carintano, charantano)

A general colloquial name for the **grosso** or **groschen**-type coin of Tyrol and Carinthia circulating in northern Italy from the 14th century. The name derives from the Italian word for 'Carinthia' (today *Carinzia*).

carlin (carlino)

An Italian gold and silver coin of the 13th to 18th centuries. The gold coin (*carlin d'or*) was first struck in about 1278 by Charles I of Anjou, King of Naples, and its name derives from him. (This coin was also known as the **salute**.) The silver coin (*carlin d'argent*) was struck in the reign of Charles's son, Charles II (1285–1309), and was modelled on the French **gros tournois**, with later forms of it appearing as the **gigliato**, **alfonsino**, and **coronato**. In southern Italy the coin survived in one form or another until as late as 1859.

carolin

A silver coin of Sweden with a value of 2 Swedish **marks** introduced in 1664 by Charles XI, whose portrait it bore and after whom it was named. In 1718 Charles XII issued coins with a value of 4, 2 and 1 carolin, the highest of which (equal to 8 marks) was known as a **ducatone**. A gold carolin was also in circulation at this time, and was first struck in the early 17th century by Charles IX. A later gold carolin was the one having a value of 10 French **francs** that was struck in 1868 by Charles XV. Compare **carlin** (above) and **carolus** (below) for similar 'Charles' coins.

carolus

The name of various coins minted in the reign of a king Charles and often bearing his Latin name CAROLUS. The two best known were the French billon coin struck in the late 15th century under Charles VIII, which was also current in England, and the English gold coin also known as a **unite** that was struck in the reign of Charles I in the 17th century. The **carolus d'or** was a name given to the low content **goldgulden** introduced in 1517 for the Spanish Netherlands by Charles V, and the **carolus d'argent** was the first Netherlands **thaler**, struck in 1543, also by Charles V, as a silver equivalent to the carolus d'or. It was also known as the carolus gulden and had a value of 20 **patards**, as the gold coin did.

carolus d'argent see **carolus**.

carolus d'or see **carolus**.

carrarino
A silver coin of Padua, Italy, struck in the 14th century by Jacopino da Carrara and his successor Francesco I da Carrara. The obverse bore a representation of a cart (Italian *carra*) to serve as a pun on the family name, while at the same time providing the colloquial name of the coin itself.

cartwheel
A nickname for the heavy copper 2-**penny** piece struck in the reign of George III by Matthew Bolton at his Soho Mint in 1797. The coin, which weighed 2 ounces, had a raised edge with an inscription, and this, combined with the hugeness of the piece, prompted the popular name.

cash (plural, same)
A common Chinese coin of copper alloy, characteristically having a square hole in the middle (so that it can be hung on thread). For a long time this was the only coin of China, and the name also came to be used generally (or loosely) for other oriental coins, such as those of southern India. The word has nothing to do with English 'cash' meaning 'ready money', 'coins and banknotes', which comes through Old French *casse*, 'cash box' from Latin *capsa*, 'chest' (and so is related to modern English 'case'), but is a European borrowing, probably through Portuguese *caixa* (which also confusingly means 'cash-box', see **caixa** above) from Tamil *kācu*, a word for a

small copper coin (compare **kas**). The Chinese themselves called the coin **tsien**, and the Russians called it *chokh*.

cassiusgroschen

A silver **groschen** of Bonn, Germany, issued in the early 14th century under Archbishop Henry II. The name derives from the view of St Cassius' church on the reverse of the coin, with this saint being the city's patron saint.

castellano

A name used for any gold coin bearing the coat of arms of the house of Castile, and in particular the 14th-century coin equal to 30 **maravedis** that was issued under Pedro I, King of Castile.

castruccino

The name of a silver coin of Lucca, Italy, with a value equal to the mezzo **grosso** that was issued in the 14th century under Castruccio Castracani degli Antelminelli, Duke of Lucca.

cavalier

The French name for coins of the Netherlands that depicted a knight on horseback on the obverse, with the Dutch name for such coins being the **rijder**. Thus the *cavalier d'or* corresponded to the *gouden rijder* and the *cavalier d'argent* was the same as the *rijderdaelder*.

cavallo

A copper coin with a value of only one two-hundredth of a **ducat**, introduced in 1472 for the kingdoms of Naples and Sicily by Ferdinand of Aragon and having a horse (Italian *cavallo*) on the reverse. Compare **cavallotto** (below).

cavallotto

A silver coin struck in the early 16th century by Louis XII of France for Asti, Italy, and bearing a figure of a horse on the reverse (compare **cavallo**, above). Other coins of this name were also struck at the same time and later in other Italian cities, such as Carmagnola and Correggio.

cedi

The basic monetary unit of Ghana introduced in 1965 and equal to 100 **pesewas**. The name is a native (Fanti) one meaning 'shell', referring to the cowries or shell money that were formerly in use among coastal tribes here.

ceitil

The first copper coin of modern Europe, introduced under John I of Portugal in 1415 and having a value of one-sixth of a **real**. Its name comes from that of Ceuta, the Spanish military town and seaport captured by the Portuguese that year.

cent

One of the most common of all international denominations and coins, in many countries being one-hundredth of a **dollar** wherever that coin is current. The name goes back through Old French to Latin *centum*, 'hundred'. See Appendix II (page 243), for many variant 'hundred' names in different countries and currencies. The most famous cent is of course that of the United States, where it was introduced in 1793.

centavo

The equivalent to the **cent**: the coin or monetary unit that is one-hundredth of a **peso** or some other denomination in several decimal currencies of Central and South America. The word is essentially the Spanish or Portuguese form of 'cent'.

centenionalis

A late Roman brass coin with a value of one-hundredth of a **solidus**. The basis is once again Latin *centum*, 'hundred'.

centesimo

A coin or unit of currency that is one-hundredth of a larger unit in Italian- or Spanish-speaking countries such as Uruguay, where it is one-hundredth of a **peso**, and Italy itself, with 100 centesimos to a **lira**. The larger unit in Panama is the **balboa**.

centime

The one-hundredth part of the French **franc**. It was introduced by the revolutionary government in 1795 as part of the new decimal system. The coin or the unit also exists or existed in many other French-speaking countries, such as Belgium and former French colonies in Africa.

centimo

The coin or monetary unit that is one-hundredth part of a larger denomination in various Latin American countries, including Venezuela and Costa Rica. In Spain, its country of origin, it is the one-hundredth part of the **peseta**.

cervia

A silver coin of Massa di Lunigiana, Italy, held by the Malaspino family in the 16th century. The obverse portrayed a stag (Italian *cervo*), but the animal was popularly supposed to be a wolf, causing the colloquial name for the coin to be *lupetta* (diminutive of *lupo*, 'wolf'). For a similar case of mistaken animal identity, see **armelino**.

chaise d'or

A gold coin of France, first struck in the 14th century and so named from the large throne (French *chaise*, 'chair') on which King Philip IV sat. The same name was used subsequently for other similar coins, including the Anglo-Gallic one copied directly from it, struck by Edward III shortly after.

chalkos

A small low-value coin of Ancient Greece, worth one-eighth of an **obol**. The coin was a copper one, and this is what the Greek name actually means.

chelin

A term used in southern Canada in the 19th century for two coins: first, the 20-**cent** piece issued in 1858, then the 25-cent piece struck in 1870. The name is a French-Canadian version of 'shilling'.

chervonetz (plural, **chervontzy**)

A name originally given in Russia to foreign gold coins, especially Dutch **ducats**. The latter were so popular in the 17th century, that in the 18th the Russians followed suit to produce their own chervontzy: originally gold ones worth 3 **roubles** struck in 1701, and later, in the 20th century, in Soviet times, banknote denominations of 1, 2, or more chervontzy, with a standard value of 1 chervonetz to 10 roubles. In 1923 only, however, the Soviet government struck gold coins again. The name refers to the colour of the original gold, and derives from Polish *czerwony*, 'gold'.

chetrum

A monetary unit of Bhutan introduced in the reform of 1974 to replace the **paisa** and **rupee**. The chetrum is one-hundredth of a **ngultrum**, and its name derives from native (Tibetan-Burmese) *che*, 'half', with *trum* short for *tram-ka*, a loanword from an Indian language, probably Hindi. There is no single chetrum coin, although there are multiples of 5, 10, 20, 25 and 50.

chetvertak

Another name for the Russian **polupoltina**, so called since it had a value of 25 **kopecks**, or a quarter (Russian *chetvert'*) of a **rouble**. Compare **chetvertina** (below).

chetvertina

An earlier type of **polupoltina** (see **chetvertak**, above), in circulation from 1654 to 1662. Like the chetvertak, it had a value of 25 **kopecks**, or a quarter of a **rouble**.

christian d'or

A Danish **pistole**, struck irregularly between 1771 and 1870 under three kings of Denmark named Christian (VII, VIII and IX).

christinchen

The German name of the Swedish coin that was worth half a **christiner** (i.e. 4 marks) and that bore the portrait of Queen Christina from 1649. The name is a diminutive, a 'little christiner'.

christiner
A silver coin of Sweden struck in the 17th century under Queen Christina and bearing her portrait. The christiner had a value of 8 Swedish **marks**. See also **christinchen** (above).

christusgulden
The name of the **goldgulden** struck in the 15th century by David of Burgundy, Bishop of Utrecht, and having a picture of Christ enthroned on the obverse.

chuckram
A small silver coin of southern India current from the 18th century and having a value of 16 **cash**, with 4 chuckram equal to 1 **fanam**. The name comes from Hindi *chakram*, itself ultimately from Sanskrit *cakra*, 'wheel' (which word also gave English 'chukka' in the sport of polo). The reference was to the shape of the coin.

cinco
The name is Spanish for 'five' and was the name for the French 5-**franc** piece in the Dominican Republic before the introduction of the **peso**, which was modelled on it.

cincuentino
The largest Spanish silver coin, struck in the 17th century and having a value of 50 (Spanish *cincuenta*) **reales**. It had a diameter of 73mm (nearly 3 inches).

cinquinho
A small silver coin of Portugal, first issued under King Emanuel (Manuel I) in the late 15th century and having a value of 5 **reis**. The name is based on the Portuguese for 'five' (*cinco*). The coin was abolished in the mid-16th century.

cistophorus
A silver coin of Ancient Greece, first issued by the kings of Pergamum in the 2nd century BC and having a value of 3 or 4 **drachmai**. The name literally means 'chest-bearer', and relates to the so-called *cista mystica*, intertwined with serpents, that was represented on it.

This was a chest (more precisely, a basket) used in the Dionysiac and other mysteries.

clementi
A papal silver coin with a value of 15 **baiocchi**, first struck under Clement VII in the 16th century and named after him.

clinckaert
The name of a gold coin of the Netherlands in circulation in the 14th and 15th centuries and resembling the **chaise d'or**, especially the Anglo-Gallic one struck by Edward III in the 14th century. The name almost certainly derives from Dutch *clincken*, 'to ring', 'to sound', referring to the distinctive ringing sound of the coin when struck or dropped.

clover cent
A popular name for the **cent** struck in 1793 in the United States, which under the bust of Liberty showed a spray of leaves resembling a clover plant.

cob
A colloquial name in Ireland in the 17th and 18th centuries, and later in some British colonies, for the Spanish **dollar** or **piece of eight**. The word was probably used to mean 'big', 'stout', since the coin was a large silver one.

collot
A colloquial name for the counterstamped **sou** of Guadeloupe, struck in 1767 for the American colonies but not circulated. The name was that of the governor of Guadeloupe in 1793 who ordered the coins to be put into circulation, Georges Henri Victor Collot.

colombiano
A 19th-century name for the Colombian **peso**.

colon (plural, **colones**)
A monetary unit of Costa Rica and El Salvador, with a value of 100 **centimos** in the former country and 100 **centavos** in the latter. The colon, named after Christopher

Columbus (in Spanish Cristóbal Colón), was introduced in Costa Rica in 1896 instead of the **peso**, and is still a coin there as well as a banknote. In El Salvador, where the denomination was first struck in 1919, also to replace the peso, the colon now exists only in note form.

colonnato
An Italian name for the **piastre** circulating in the Middle East in the 17th century and so called for the representation of the Pillars of Hercules (the two promontories at the east end of the Strait of Gibraltar) on the reverse, from Italian *colonnato*, 'colonnade'.

conant
A colloquial name for the silver **peso** of the Philippines introduced in 1903 on the recommendation of the American banking expert, Charles A. Conant.

condor
A gold or silver coin of certain South American countries with a value of 10 **pesos**. It was first introduced in Chile (as a gold coin) in 1851, and as originally struck bore the portrayal of a condor as a symbol of strength to mark the country's political independence from Spain. Later coins of the name, such as those struck in Colombia and Ecuador, carried a figure or head of Liberty on one side and the country's coat of arms or the value on the other. The Ecuador condor was worth 25 **sucres**.

constantin d'or
A name for the **pistole** or double **ducat** issued in the second half of the 18th century by Ludwig Constantin von Rohan-Montbazon, Bishop of Strasbourg (then part of Germany but now in France).

conto
Before 1942, the name of a monetary unit of Brazil equal to 1000 **milreis**. The name, which is Portuguese for 'number', was also used to apply to the value of 1000 **cruzeiros** after this date, since this was the currency that superseded the milreis. In Portugal itself the name was and still is current to mean 1000 **escudos**.

conventionstaler

A **thaler** struck according to the monetary convention of 1753 between Austria and Bavaria, which decreed that 2 **gulden** were equal to 1 thaler. The coin itself usually bore the Latin inscription AD NORMAM CONVENTIONIS ('to the standard of the convention'). The best known of the denomination after 1780 was the widely circulating **Maria Theresa thaler**.

copkini (cophini)

A Netherlands **pfennig** struck by Florence IV of Holland in the 13th century. The name is an early Dutch word meaning 'head', referring to the bare head of the monarch on the obverse of the coin. The copkini was in circulation in the Lower Rhine district down to the beginning of the 14th century, and was there called by its German name of *Köpfchen*.

coquibus

A billon coin struck in the early 14th century by Guy II, Bishop of Cambrai and subsequently copied by William I of Hainaut. The coin had a rough figure of an eagle on the obverse, but this was popularly taken to be a cock, hence the name.

cordoba

The chief monetary unit of Nicaragua, equal to 100 **centavos** and introduced in 1912. It is named after Hernández de Córdoba, the 16th-century Spanish governor of Nicaragua who took possession of that country in 1522.

coroa de prata

The name of the Portuguese **thaler**, worth 1000 **reales**, that was introduced in 1835 on the adoption of a decimal system of currency. The words are Portuguese for 'silver crown'. When the gold standard was introduced in 1854 the coin ceased to be struck. Compare **coroa d'ouro** (below).

coroa d'ouro

The Portuguese 'gold crown' that was introduced in 1822 with a value of 5000 **reales**. Compare **coroa de prata** (above).

corona

The Latin word meaning 'crown' that was a symbol of sovereignty and that gave the basis for the various coins known as **crown** or the equivalent. (See in particular **korona**.) No actual Roman coins were called by the name, but there were several coins that bore different representations of crowns or crowned heads (often in the form of a laurel wreath).

coronato

The name of a billon coin of Castile struck in the 13th century under Sancho IV and bearing his crowned head. In the 15th century, the same name was in use for a **grosso** of Ferdinand I of Naples, which portrayed his coronation at Barletta.

coronilla

The name is Spanish for 'small crown', and was a general nickname for several Spanish gold coins having a crown on the reverse, especially the half-**escudo**.

couronne

The French for 'crown' and a general name for the **écu** and for similar coins bearing a crown. (Compare **coronilla**, above.)

crimbal

A silver coin with a value of 6 or 12 **sols** that was issued in 1731 by the French government for circulation in the Windward Islands (Îles du Vent), in the West Indies. The coin was introduced to Barbados by an Englishman called Crimbal and thus acquired its name from him there.

crocard (crockard)

A base metal coin like the **pollard**, imported from the continent to England in the late 13th century, and probably circulating with a value of 2 to a **penny**. It was banned, however, after 1310. Its name is of uncertain origin but could relate to French *croc*, 'hook', 'crook', perhaps since it could be easily bent (compare **crookie**, below).

crookie

The name is a former Scottish slang term for a **sixpence**, given since the coin was easily 'crooked' or bent. Hence the 'crooked sixpence' of the nursery rhyme.

crown

One of the most famous of English coins, with its name obviously referring to the royal crown it bore. The first coin of the name was the so-called 'crown of the rose', a gold coin struck under Wolsey in 1526 and modelled on the French **écu au soleil**. Its value was 4 **shillings** and 6 **pence**, and its obverse bore a shield with a crown over it, while the reverse had a large cross over a rose. The same year it was superseded by the 'crown of the double rose', with a value of 5 shillings, and this gold coin was supplemented in 1551 by a silver crown, still with a value of 5 shillings. In recent times, with one exception, crowns have been struck only as commemorative pieces, the single exception being the Churchill crown of 1965 (although even that has now become a collectors' piece). Compare **half-crown**.

cruzado (crusado)

A gold coin of Portugal with an original value of 400 **reis**, first struck under Alfonso V in 1457. Its name derives from Portuguese *cruzar*, 'to cross', 'mark with a cross', with reference to the large cross on the reverse. Compare **cruzeiro** (below).

cruzeiro

A coin of Brazil with a value of 100 **centavos**, introduced in 1942 in place of the **milreis**. As with the much earlier **cruzado**, the name is based on Portuguese *cruz*, 'cross', and refers to the prominent cross on the reverse.

cuarenta

A silver coin of Cuba introduced in 1915. Its name is that of its value of 40 **centavos** (Spanish *cuarenta*, 'forty').

cuartilla

A former small coin of Mexico, worth a quarter of a **real** and in circulation from 1810 to 1863. Its name relates to its value (from Spanish *cuarto*, 'quarter'). Compare **cuartillo** (below).

cuartillo

Originally a Spanish billon coin worth a quarter of a **real** and struck in 1566. In the 19th century the name, which simply means 'quarter', applied to various copper coins struck in Central and South America, for example in San Domingo and Colombia. Compare **cuartilla** (above) and **cuartino** (below).

cuartino

A copper coin of Venezuela struck in 1822 and worth a quarter of a **real**. Like the **cuartilla** and **cuartillo** (above), the name is based on Spanish *cuarto*, 'quarter'.

cuarto

A copper coin of Spain worth a quarter of a **real**, first struck under Ferdinand V and Isabella (1471–1504). The name is simply Spanish for 'quarter'.

cuatro

A silver coin of Bolivia circulating in the mid-19th century with a value of 4 **reals**. Its name is simply Spanish for 'four'.

D

daalder

A large silver coin of Brabant (Netherlands) introduced originally as a presentation piece in the reign of Charles V (1519–56) and as currency under his son Philip II (1556–98). In the northern provinces of the Netherlands it was worth 2 Dutch **gulden** (**guilders**) and in the southern provinces 32 **patards**. The coin's name is the Dutch equivalent of **thaler**, from its resemblance to the German coin so called.

dala

A silver coin of Hawaii struck (in San Francisco) for King David Kalakaua in 1883. The name is a 'bastardised' form of **dollar**.

dalar

A Polish coin equivalent to the **thaler**, as its name implies. It had a value of 30 **groschen** (otherwise **groszy**) and was originally struck under Sigismund III (1587–1632).

daldre

The name of the **daalder** in the southern provinces of the Netherlands, with 'daldre' as a dialect variant of the more widely used name.

daler

A copper coin of Sweden circulating in the 17th and 18th centuries and based on the German **thaler**, hence its name.

danaretto (denaretto)

A small Venetian coin issued under the Doges of Venice from the 12th to the 14th centuries as a reduced version of the **denaro**, so that its name means simply 'little denaro'.

dandyprat

The colloquial name of a number of small English coins of the past, but especially the half-**groat** struck under Henry VII (1485–1509) and a 1½-**pence** piece issued under Elizabeth a century later. The name was adopted from the existing word already in use to mean 'dwarf', 'small boy', 'insignificant person', but having an unknown origin. The coin was also known as a **dodkin** (see **doit**).

danielstaler

A **thaler** struck in 1561 by Princess Maria of Jever, and bearing on the reverse a representation of the prophet Daniel surrounded by four lions.

daric

A standard gold coin of the Persian empire, forming with the **siglos** the chief currency of Asia when it was under Persian domination, down to the time of Alexander the Great in the 4th century BC. The daric was first struck under Darius the Great (521–486 BC) and is almost certainly named after him.

dauphin

A billon coin of France struck specially for the ancient province of Dauphiné. The *petit dauphin* was issued under Charles V (1364–80) and the *grand dauphin* under Charles VII (1422–61).

davidsgulden

A type of gold **gulden** struck in the Netherlands at Utrecht under Bishop David of Burgundy (1456–96) and bearing a portrait of the biblical King David as a harpist on the obverse.

decadrachm

A large silver coin of Ancient Greece having a value of 10 **drachmai**, hence its name. It was issued only on special occasions and was in effect more of a medallion than a coin proper.

decenario

A type of mezzo **grosso** ('medium grosso') struck in Merano by the Counts of Tyrol and having a value of 10 **piccolos**. Hence its name, based on Italian *dieci*, 'ten'.

décime

The name given to the 10-**cent** piece in the French decimal currency of the late 18th century. When the **franc** was introduced in 1803, the décime acquired the value of one-tenth of a franc. The coin itself is no longer struck.

decimo

The name given to a coin equal to 10 **centavos** in the 19th century in a number of South American countries that had adopted a decimal system of currency.

decus

The colloquial name in the 17th century for the English **crown** piece, deriving as the first word of its edge inscription: DECUS ET TUTAMEN, 'An ornament and a safeguard'. (This describes the double purpose of the inscription itself, as both decorative and a guard against 'clipping' or other physical damage.) This same inscription reappeared on the edge of the first British **pound** coin, struck in 1983, as a specifically 'English' issue. (In 1984 the coin was struck in a Scottish issue, and the inscription changed to: NEMO ME IMPUNE LACESSIT, 'No one provokes me with impunity', the motto of the Order of the Thistle and of the kings of Scotland. In 1985, the Welsh issue had the inscription: PLEIDIOL WYF I'M GWLAD, 'True am I to my country'. In 1986, the Northern Ireland issue returned with the DECUS inscription, as did the 1987 English one.) Despite certain public interest in the wording and its meaning, the modern coin was not called a 'decus' as its predecessor had been three hundred years earlier.

decussis

A large copper coin of Ancient Rome having a value of 10 **asses**, as its name indicates (from Latin *decem*, 'ten' and *as*). The coin was in circulation in the 3rd century BC and bore no inscription but merely a figure 'X' on the reverse (together with a ship's prow).

demy

A Scottish gold coin first struck in the late 14th century under Robert III and having a value of half a **crown**, hence its name.

denarino

A silver coin of Modena, Italy, struck in the 16th century and equal to half a **soldo**. Its name means 'little denaro' (compare **danaretto**).

denarius

The main coin of Ancient Rome in Republican and Imperial times, when it superseded the **quadrigatus** and **victoriatus**. It was originally a silver coin worth 10 **asses**, hence its name, which means 'containing ten'. It gradually became more and more debased, however, until it was eventually a bronze coin and was in turn superseded by the **antoninianus** (although it was revived in the 3rd century AD under Diocletian as the **argenteus**). The so-called '**penny**' of the Bible (in the New Testament) was the original silver denarius. The coin, and name, influenced much of the subsequent coinage of Europe and was the prototype of the **denier**, **denaro** and **dinar**, for example, as well as the letter 'd' of English 'L.S.D.' (or '£.s.d.'), meaning formerly 'pounds, shillings and pence', and hence colloquially 'money'.

denaro

The Italian version of the **denier**, based directly on the Roman **denarius**, as reintroduced into Europe by Charlemagne. (See **denier** for more on this.)

denezhka

The name of the Russian copper coin of the 19th century that was worth half a **kopeck**, with the name itself a diminutive of **denga** (see next entry).

denga

The main and in some provinces only coin of Russia first struck in the late 14th century and originally having a value of one two-hundredth of a **grivna**, or 1 **rouble**. At first a silver coin, by the 18th century it had become a debased copper piece worth only one **kopeck**. It ceased to be struck in 1828 but minting was resumed in 1839 when, retaining its old name, the coin was worth simply half a kopeck. (It was popularly called the **denezhka**, and soon this name actually appeared on it.) The name is ultimately of Tatar origin, meaning 'silver coin', and the plural of the term (today properly spelt *den'gi*) is now the standard Russian word for 'money'. Compare **denning** (below) and, as a related name, **tankah**.

denier

The standard silver coin of western Europe, based directly on the Roman **denarius** and introduced to Europe by Charlemagne in the 8th century. He divided the silver **pound** (**libra**) into 20 **sols** (**solidi**), each worth 12 deniers. In this way, 240 deniers were struck from one pound of fine silver. (Hence, too, the original English monetary system, with 12 **pence** to the **shilling**, and 240 pence to the pound.) The denier eventually became a very small copper coin, and ceased to be struck under Louis XVI in the late 18th century. The English silver penny was based closely on the original denier.

denning

A silver coin of Denmark based on the Russian **denga**, struck at Copenhagen in 1619. The name is a danicised version of the Russian name.

deutschmark (deutsche mark)

The standard monetary unit of West Germany, literally 'German **mark**', instituted in 1948 and so called to distinguish it from the East German mark (which was also originally known by this name but later became first *Mark der Deutschen Notenbank*, 'mark of the German issuing bank' and then, from 1968, *Mark der Deutschen Demokratischen Republik*, 'mark of the German Democratic Republic'). The deutschmark is usually abbreviated to 'DM' in financial statements.

deventergans

A nickname for the **grosso** issued in Deventer, Netherlands, by Frederick von Blankenheim, Bishop of Utrecht (1393–1423). The name literally means 'Deventer goose'

63

and refers to the poorly executed representation of an eagle on the reverse.

diamante

A silver coin of Ferrara, corresponding to the **grosso**. It was struck in the mid-15th century and derives its name from the figure of a diamond on the obverse.

dicken

Literally, a 'thick' coin. The name applies to certain silver coins that were imitations of the Italian **testone** only thicker and heavier. They were, moreover, 'thick' by contrast with the much thinner and lighter **kreuzers** and **pfennigs**. The oldest known dicken was struck in Berne in 1492.

didrachm

As its name suggests, a coin of Ancient Greece worth 2 **drachmai**. It was not as common as the **tetradrachm**, which was twice its value.

dime

The well-known American silver coin with a value of 10 **cents** (one-tenth of a **dollar**). It was struck in 1796, but its name was devised earlier, in 1785, and was based by President-to-be Jefferson on French *dixième*, 'tenth', with the word originally spelt 'disme' and pronounced 'deem'. The spelling and pronunciation were subsequently modified to their present forms.

dinar

An Arab gold coin originally struck in the 7th century in Syria by Abd-al-Malik, Caliph of Damascus, with its name based on the Roman **denarius** (more precisely, the *denarius aureus* of Byzantium). The original value of the dinar was 10 **dirhams**, although later issues had differing values. Today the dinar is the monetary unit of several countries, including Bahrain, Iraq, Jordan and Kuwait (where it has a value of 1000 **fils**), Algeria (1000 **centimes**) and Yugoslavia (100 **paras**). In Libya its value is 1000 dirhams.

dinero

A Spanish silver coin based on the Roman **denarius** and first struck in the 11th century (originally as a billon coin, but as a proper silver coin in the 13th century under Ferdinand III). In more recent times, the name has applied to the 10-**centavo** coin of Peru introduced in 1857.

dinheiro

A Portuguese coin that was the equivalent of the **denier**, in circulation from the 12th to the 14th centuries. Unlike the denier, however, it was a billon coin.

diobol

A silver coin of Ancient Greece with a value of one-third of a **drachma** or, as its name indicates, 2 **obols**.

dirham (dirhem)

An Arab silver coin similar in type to the **dinar** and still existing as a nickel coin (since 1965, earlier silver) of Morocco, where it has a value of 100 **centimes**. The name is an Arabic version of Greek **drachma**. Today the dirham is also the main currency of the United Arab Emirates, where it is divided into 10 dinars, or 1000 **fils**.

dizain

A French coin of the 15th and 16th centuries worth 10 **deniers**, and thus part of an early experiment at decimalisation. The dizain (from French *dix*, 'ten') lost out to the duodecimal coinage established by Francis I in 1540, and during its currency was regarded as 'awkward' by comparison with the 12-denier **douzain** and 6-denier **sixain**. (It would have been like a fivepenny piece in the old predecimal English currency, with its familiar **shillings** and **sixpences**.)

dobla

The word is Spanish for 'double', and the name was that of a number of gold coins with a value of double some denomination or other, such as the double **ducat** struck in the 16th century by Charles V for Naples and Sicily, or the contemporary double **scudo** struck in Genoa. As a Spanish coin pure and simple, the dobla was first struck in the 14th century under Alfonso XI, and this was copied in a variety of types to the 15th century, when multiple doblas were also minted. Compare **doblado**, **doblone** and **doubloon** (below).

doblado

This was not only an alternative name for the **dobla** (above), but also the independent name of two coins of Argentina and Ecuador. In the former country, it was a gold coin worth 2 **escudos**, struck from 1824 to 1890. In Ecuador, the doblado was struck from 1835 with an identical value.

dobler

A copper coin of Majorca (Mallorca) current to 1750 and having a value of 2 **dineros**. The name is one of the 'double' family (see **dobla**, above).

doblone

The name of various gold coins of Italy, but especially those having a value of 4 **scudi** struck in Bologna and the Vatican in the 16th century and a value of 8 scudi struck at Modena. From these values, it can be seen that the denomination was more a multiple than an exact double, as the name implies.

dobra

A gold coin of Portugal first struck in the 14th century under Pedro I. Like the names immediately above, the meaning is 'double', although the value of the coin was more multiple than exactly twice a particular denomination. The original dobra was in fact closely based on the French **écu d'or**. By the 19th century, the dobra that had been reintroduced by John V in 1722 had come to be worth as much as 16,000 **reis**.

dodecadrachm

The largest coin of Ancient Greece, having a value, as its name indicates, of 12 **drachmai**. It was struck in Carthage from 237 BC.

dodkin

A colloquial early name for the **doit** in the 15th century, indicating a 'little doit' (as it were a 'doitkin'). The name was also used on occasions to apply to any small coin. Compare **dandyprat** (above).

dog

A colloquial name for the Dutch **leeuwendaalder** when it was in circulation in Maryland (later in the USA) in about 1700. The reference was to the lion on the coin, which was popularly taken to be a dog.

doit

A small copper coin of the Netherlands current from the late 16th century to the early 19th, and having a value of 2 **pfennigs**, or one-eighth of a **stuiver**. The coin came to be used for small change in England and the name acquired the general sense 'small sum' (as did '**farthing**', for example). The word itself derives from Middle Dutch *duit*, 'small coin', itself ultimately related to the English verb 'whittle'.

dollar

One of the best known of all coins, whose name and history is closely bound up with that of the **thaler** (with 'dollar' thus an American form and pronunciation of this earlier coin). The dollar was first authorised for minting in 1792, although it was not struck until two years later. Its equivalent in the South American states is the **peso**. The familiar dollar sign ($) probably developed as a variant of the former Spanish contraction for the peso or **piece of eight**, which would have been a figure '8' between two sloping lines, thus: /8/. In more modern times the double lines are often streamlined to just one (vertically through the centre of the '8').

dominicano

A 'ghost' coin of the Dominican Republic, which was to have been introduced in 1889 but which was never struck (for economic reasons, since the country was then still dependent on the United States). There would have been 100 **centesimos** to the dominicano and the coin itself would have been a silver one, with higher multiples (25, 50 and 100) as gold coins.

dong (plural, same)
A bronze coin of Indo-China (Annam, today Vietnam) dating back to the 10th century. It was based on the Chinese **cash** and had the same central square hole. The meaning of the name can be seen in the inscription on the obverse: *thong bun*, i.e. 'current coin'. Today's coin is made not from bronze but from an alloy (copper/pewter/zinc).

doppelchen
A colloquial German name for the 2-**pfennig** piece (properly *doppelpfennig*) or the half-**kreuzer** issued under the Electors of Trier in the 18th century.

doppia
A name (literally 'double') used for various coins issued in different Italian states at different times, when it had a value of twice some standard denomination such as the **ducat** or the **scudo**. The doppia that was a double ducat, for example, was a gold coin first struck in Milan in the 15th century under Galeazzo Maria Sforza, Duke of Milan. The name was also one used by Italians for the Spanish double **escudo** (known in English as the **doubloon**) which appeared in Italy from about 1500 and virtually ousted the Italian double ducat.

doppietta
A small gold coin struck by the Dukes of Savoy in 1768 and 1773. Its name derives as a diminutive of **doppia** (see above), which it resembled. Its value, however, was not a double one but equalled 5 Sardinian **lire**, or one-fifth of a **carlino**.

dornenkranztaler
Literally a 'crown of thorns **thaler**', the name of the thaler struck by Maria von Jever in the 16th century. Maria was a great coin-issuer, and this piece was designed to be a kind of visual representation of the difficulties encountered by 'Fräulein von Jever', as she

was known, in her official duties. The obverse of the coin bore the family crest, and the reverse a crown of thorns.

double

The name of several coins that had a value of twice a standard denomination, such as the French silver coin current from the 14th century that was a double **denier** (worth one-sixth of a **sol**) and, in the Anglo-Gallic series, a double **gros**. Other well known 'double' coins were the double **crown** (which see), the American double **eagle**, or 20-**dollar** gold piece first struck in the mid-19th century, the double **lorrain** (a special version of the double **tournois** struck for Lorraine in the 17th century), and the double tournois itself, this being a small copper coin of France struck from 1577 onwards with a value of two deniers. 'Double' was also the name of a copper coin of Guernsey, introduced in 1830 at a value of half a **farthing**. In this case it was the larger denomination that was double the smaller, and Guernsey farthings were also known as 'two doubles'.

doubloon

The name, with its historical and romantic overtones (although not as much as **pieces of eight**), is the English rendering of Spanish *doblón*, via French *doublon*, itself directly based on **dobla**, 'double' (see this separately) and in effect meaning 'large **double**'. Although the name has been used loosely in English for various Spanish-Mexican coins that circulated in England and Europe generally from the 16th century to the 18th, the word particularly applied to the double **escudo**, which was also widely known as the **pistole**. The piece was first struck in 1537 under Charles V (Charles I of Spain).

douzain

The name clearly implies 'twelve', and was that of a French billon coin with a value of one-twelfth of a silver **franc**, and later of an **écu**. It was first struck under Charles VIII in the late 15th century. There were several subsequent coins of the same name, including those issued under Louis XII (1498–1515) and Francis I (1515–47).

69

drachma (plural, **drachmai**)

This was the basic silver coin of Ancient Greece, where it was also the name of a standard weight, as it still is in many countries today (in English as 'drachm'). The derivation of the word is in Greek *dragma*, 'handful', pointing to the original concept of a handful of **obols**, subsequently standardised as 6 in number. (Historically this dates back to the earliest times, when currency was not organised in coinage but in square metal bars, and it would have been a handful of such bars that made the original drachma.) Today, the Greek drachma has a value of 100 **lepta**.

drake

A colloquial name in England for the silver **shilling** minted in the 17th century under Elizabeth. The coin had a martlet as its mintmark, and this heraldic bird was the origin of the 'drake' of the name.

dreibätzner

A 'three-**batz**' coin struck in Austria and southern Germany in the 16th century, where the silver piece was the main denomination together with the *Sechsbaetzner* ('six-batz' coin), double it in value.

dreibrüdertaler

The 'three-brother-**thaler**', a nickname for those thalers that bore portraits of three brothers of any reigning house, such as the Electors of Saxony Christian II, John-George (Johann-Georg) I and Augustus (1591–1611), or the three brothers who were Dukes of Silesia, George (Georg), Ludwig and Christian (1653–69), and whose portraits appeared on the **reichstaler** issued in 1656.

dreier

A 'three-er', otherwise a common name for the base silver coin worth 3 **pfennigs** or 3 **kreuzer** that was struck in a number of German states from the 16th century. Compare **sechser**.

dreigröscher
A colloquial name for the triple **groschen** struck in the 16th century in Poland, Lithuania and some parts of Prussia.

dreikaisertaler
A name popularly used for the **thaler** struck under Ferdinand I in the mid-16th century and bearing the three crowned busts of himself, Maximilian I and Charles V.

dreiling
A billon coin worth 3 **pfennigs** that was struck in Hamburg and Lübeck from the early 15th century. Unusually, the coin did not bear the figure '3' but the total number of the coins which made up 1 **reichstaler** (originally 128, but later 192).

dreipölker
A 'three-*Pölchen*' coin, that is, the German name of a Polish coin that was itself based on the German **groschen**, and that had a value of $1\frac{1}{2}$ groschen in Germany. (*Pölchen* was the German diminutive of Polish *pol*, 'half'.) The name was also used of the **poltorak** struck from 1614 in imitation of this coin itself.

dreizehner
A 'thirteener', the colloquial name of a silver coin of Dortmund struck in the 17th century bearing a figure '13' to denote its value of one-thirteenth of a **thaler**.

drielander (incorrectly, **dreilander**)
A colloquial Dutch name (based on *drie*, 'three' and *land*) for a coin with a value of a double **gros** that was issued in the early 15th century in Brabant, Holland and Hainaut.

drittel
Literally a 'third', the name of a coin worth one-third of a **thaler** that was struck in the second half of the 17th century in accordance with the Zinne monetary standard of 1667.

71

dritthalber

A 'two-and-a-halfer', otherwise a colloquial German name in the 18th century for a coin that had a value of 2½ times some accepted denomination or other. Among them were the Bremen dritthalber worth 2½ **schwaren**, the Franconian coin worth 2½ **kreuzers**, and the Brunswick (Braunschweig) piece with a value of 2½ **pfennigs**.

duarius

A Latin name meaning 'relating to two' used generally for the base silver 2-**kreuzer** coins struck for Hungary and Transylvania from the 16th century to the 18th.

dub

A small copper coin formerly current in parts of India, with its name an English simplification of the native word for 'coin', Telugu *ḍabbu* or Marathi *ḍhabbū*.

ducat

A well-known gold or silver coin (usually gold) circulating in many forms in various parts of Europe for a fairly lengthy period. The first (silver) ducat was the one minted by Roger II of Sicily for his Duchy of Apulia in about 1140. It bore the inscription 'R DX AP', i.e. *Rogerus Dux Apuliae* ('Roger Duke of Apulia'), with the middle word here giving the original germ of 'ducat'. In 1284 the first gold ducat was issued in Venice, and this bore the Latin motto (in abbreviated form): SIT. T. XTE. D. Q. T. V. REG. ISTE. DUCAT, standing for *Sit Tibi, Christe, Datus/Quem Tu Regis, Iste Ducatus* ('Unto Thee, O Christ, be dedicated this Duchy which Thou rulest'). Here, the Latin abbreviation for 'duchy' established the name of the coin, which also came to be known as a **zecchino** d'oro.

ducatone

A name meaning 'large **ducat**' in Italian, and used for a large silver coin, equivalent to a gold **scudo**, that was struck in Milan, Savoy and Venice in the second half of the 16th century. Its value was 5 **lire**, 12 **soldi**.

ducatoon

A large silver coin of the Netherlands, struck from the end of the 16th century to the end of the 18th. It was so named since its silver value was (in theory) the same as that of the gold **ducat**. Compare also **ducatone** (above).

duit

The Dutch spelling of the coin known in English as the **doit** (which see).

dump

A colloquial name used fairly generally for any coin that was small and thick, such as the first issues of **halfpennies** and **farthings** under George I (1714–27), or the small silver token current in New South Wales, Australia in the time of George III (1760–1820) (for more about this, see **holey dollar**).

duplone

A gold coin of Switzerland struck between 1787 and 1829 and having a value of 19 **francs** or 2 **ducats**. The latter is reflected in its Italian name, meaning literally 'big double'.

dupondius

A 2-**as** bronze coin of Ancient Rome, originating in southern Italy rather than Rome itself. Its name is Latin for 'two weights', 'double weight', since this was the source (as a weight) of a word that could subsequently apply to a coin having a value of double some denomination.

duro

A name sometimes used for the Spanish-American **peso** or **piece of eight**. It derives from the full form of *peso duro*, literally 'hard weight', and actually appeared on a coin minted in 1808. See **peso** for more regarding the history of the coin and its name.

düttchen

A name used for various Polish **trojaks** (triple **groschen**) circulating in southern Germany and Hungary in the late 16th century. The name is a German variant of the coin's

Polish name *dudek*. This means 'hoopoe' and seems to have derived as a popular interpretation of the imperial eagle that was represented on the coin.

dwojak
The Polish name of a 2-**groschen** piece. Compare **trojak**.

E

eagle

The name was proposed in 1785 by President-to-be Jefferson for the 10-**dollar** coin introduced in the United States in 1795. At first, the representation of the eagle on the reverse was informal, but from 1797 a heraldic type appeared. (The eagle itself is the so called American eagle, the 'eagle displayed' of heraldry, which was adopted as an emblem by the United States.) The 20-dollar coin was called the double eagle (see **double**). The eagle itself was not minted after 1933.

ebenezer

The colloquial name of the double **krone** or 8-**mark** coin struck in Denmark by Frederick III in 1569. The name derives from the inscription on the obverse, which was DOMINVS PROVIDEBIT ('The Lord will provide') and, separately, EBENEZER. The latter refers to the memorial stone mentioned in the Bible (see I Samuel 4 : 1 and 7 : 12), with the name itself interpreted as 'stone of help'.

écu

The name is French for 'shield' (from Latin *scutum*), and the coin was the French 'crown' or 'dollar', as it were, that corresponded to the Spanish **escudo**, Italian **scudo**, and Dutch **schild**. The coin was usually a gold one and was current for many years in various types and at various values, with the earliest piece struck under Louis IX in the 13th century. Among the different versions, two of the best known were the *écu d'or* struck under Philip VI in the 14th century, showing the king under a canopy on the obverse, and a shield and crown on the reverse, and the *écu d'argent*, a large silver piece (also called an *écu blanc*) first issued by Louis XIII in 1641, with a value of 3 **livres** or 60 **sols**. The *écu du soleil* ('sun shield') struck under Louis XI in the 15th century had a reverse that was copied by Henry VIII when he issued the **crown** of the rose. The name écu existed as recently as the 19th century for the French 5-**franc** coin, even though this was a decimal piece, while in more recent times, the name appears to have influenced that of the ECU (European Currency Unit), the money of account introduced in the Common Market in 1972 to settle debts between member countries and act as a standard in floating currencies. For a currency of similar international concept, see **spesmilo** and **stelo**.

engeltaler

The 'angel **thaler**', a colloquial name for the large base coin of Saxony that was issued from 1621 to 1623. The obverse bore the figure of an angel and a crest; the reverse had two angels and three crests.

engenhoso

A gold coin of Portugal first struck in 1562 by King Sebastian. The piece was the first to be struck by machinery, hence the name, which is Portuguese for 'ingenious' (literally, 'engineered'). The value of the engenhoso was 500 **reals**.

enrique

A Spanish gold coin first struck under Henry (Enrique) IV in the second half of the 15th century and named after him. The obverse showed the King enthroned; the reverse bore his name in Latin, ENRICUS. The name was an official one, and coins were struck in a range of values, from half an enrique to 50. (The latter weighed 229 grammes, or half a pound.) Compare **henri d'or**.

escalin

A silver coin of the Netherlands, current in the early 17th century and approximately equivalent to the English **shilling**, as its name indicates. (The form here is the French one, derived from Dutch *schelling*.) Compare **scalding**.

escudillo

The name is Spanish for 'little shield', or more precisely here, 'little **escudo**'. The escudillo was a Spanish gold coin of the 18th century having a value of half an escudo. It was also known as a *coronilla* ('little crown').

escudo

The name is Spanish for 'shield', and like the French **écu** (see above) the coin so designated was one of a number of gold or silver denominations current from the 16th century. The first gold coin of the name was the one minted in 1537 to supersede the **excelente**. The 'shield' was the Spanish coat of arms that appeared on the obverse. There was also a Portuguese escudo from the 18th century, and the name still exists as that of the basic currency of Portugal, as well as that of Cape Verde and, until recently (1977), Angola, a former Portuguese colony. The modern escudo is a bronze coin, however.

espadin

A billon coin of Portugal issued under Alfonso V (1438–81) to commemorate the Order of the Sword (Portuguese *espada*) instituted in 1459. The name was also that of a Portuguese gold coin struck a little later, under John II (1487–95), having a value of half a **justo**.

esphera

A gold coin of the early 16th century struck in Goa (Portuguese India), and named after the representation of the world's sphere (Portuguese *esphera*, modern *esfera*) on the reverse.

etschkreuzer

A silver coin originally struck in 1271 by Meinhard II, Count of the Tyrol, in Merano. The piece was named a **Kreuzer** from the cross that appeared on the reverse. The first part of the name, Etsch, is that of the region surrounding Merano (actually that of the river there, more usually known as Adige).

excelente

A gold coin of Spain struck in the 15th century under Ferdinand and Isabella and circulating unchanged until

1537. In size and gold content it equalled a **ducat**, having a value of 11 **reals**, 1 **maravedi**. Its name relates to its fine appearance and quality. It was superseded in 1537 by the **escudo**.

eyrir (plural, **aurar**)

The smallest currency unit of Iceland, equal to one-hundredth of a **kron**. It was first struck as a coin in the early 20th century and down to 1944 was equated with Danish currency, since Iceland was in personal union with Denmark until this date. When Iceland became an independent republic, the coin continued to be struck, although with the Icelandic crest on the obverse instead of the royal monogram. Its name is Icelandic for 'ounce', and probably ultimately derives from Latin *aureus*, 'gold coin'. Today there are no longer single eyrir coins, although there are multiples (aurar).

F

fals (fels) (plural, **falus**)
An early Arab copper coin, whose name derives from
Latin *follis*, 'money bag' (see this word as a coin name).
The word came to apply generally to copper coins struck
in the Islamic Empire at different times, and survived
until the 19th century for the copper coins of Persia.

fanam
A small gold coin of India first issued in the 9th century
and in Ceylon from the 14th. From the 16th century the
name was that of a silver coin, and this denomination
was adopted by the English to equal one-eighth of a
rupee in southern India. The word is a corruption of
Malayalam and Tamil *paṇam*, itself deriving from
Sanskrit *paṇa*, 'wealth'.

farthing
A former bronze coin of England, although originally a
silver one, first struck under Edward I in 1279. (The first
copper farthing was minted in 1672.) The name literally
means 'fourthling', since in the earliest times, the silver
penny could be cut physically into two or four parts to
give smaller value pieces, respectively **halfpennies** and
farthings. (The penny had a cross on the reverse, and the
cuts were made along the arms of this.) The bronze
farthing first appeared in 1860, and the denomination
ceased to be struck in 1956, although farthings remained
legal tender until 1961.

faruki
The name of a gold **pagoda** of Mysore issued in the late
18th century by Tipu Sahib, Sultan of Mysore. The coin

was named after Omar Faruk, the second caliph (*khalifa*).

fels see **fals**.

fen see **fun**.

fenig

The Polish name, corresponding to **pfennig**, of coins struck under the German Empire in 1917 and 1918, and intended for the proposed Kingdom of Poland. Coins with a value of 1, 5, 10 and 20 fenigs were minted, but because of the altered political situation at the end of the First World War none of the 170 million coins struck were ever issued.

ferding

A silver coin of Sweden, first struck for the Bishop of Dorpat in 1528 and later by Erik XIV, King of Sweden (1560–68) after the conquest of Estland (Estonia). The coin had a value of a quarter of a **mark**, and the origin of the name is basically the same as that of the **farthing**, since the coin was worth a fourth part of the main denomination.

fert

A gold coin of Savoy struck by Duke Lodovico (1439–65). On somewhat doubtful authority, the name is said to derive from the first letters of the family motto, 'Fortitudo Eius Rhodum Tenuit' ('He held Rhodes by his bravery'). However, the same name was given to the coin with a value of 10 **scudi** d'oro issued under Victor Amadeus I (1630–7), since this bore the legend FOEDERE ET RELIGIONE TENEMUS ('We hold by treaty and religion'), and the initial letters of this certainly spell out the coin name.

fiddler

A former English colloquial name for the **sixpence**, possibly referring to the practice of paying a fiddler this amount when he played at a dance, with each couple contributing. The word 'fiddler' (for the player) was usually understood to mean a man who specifically did so for hire, hence such phrases, common in the 17th and 18th centuries, as 'fiddler's pay', 'fiddler's money' and so on.

filiberto
A gold coin of Savoy, introduced by Emmanuel Philibert, Duke of Savoy (1553–80) and named after him. It had a value of 9 **lire**.

filippo
A silver **thaler**-type (or **crown**-type) coin first struck under Philip II of Spain for Milan in 1598, and named after him. The filippo continued to be struck at irregular intervals under other rulers until 1776.

filippone
The name of a base silver **piccolo** struck under Philip I, Count of Savoy, in the late 13th century and named after him.

filler
A low-value coin of Hungary corresponding to the **heller**, hence its name. In 1892 it was worth one-hundredth of an Austrian **krone**, in 1925 one-hundredth of a **pengo**, and currently is one-hundredth of a **forint**.

fils
A low-value coin of Middle Eastern countries such as Iraq, Bahrain, Jordan and South Yemen, in all of which it is one-thousandth of a **dinar**. The name is exactly the same as the Arabic **fals** (which see).

fisca
A small silver coin of the Canary Islands struck in 1823 at the value of one-tenth of a **peso**. When a **peseta**-based monetary system was introduced in Spain in 1868, the fisca was no longer minted. Its name is based on Spanish *fisco*, 'exchequer'.

fledermaus
The German word for 'bat', and a nickname for the **groschel** of Silesia and base silver **kreuzer** of Prussia struck in the early 19th century. Both these coins bore

81

the figure of an eagle, and this was mistakenly (or humorously) taken to be a bat.

florenus de camera

A gold papal coin corresponding to the Florentine **florin** that was struck in Avignon in the second half of the 14th century. The Latin name means 'florin of the [Papal] Palace', and the coin was issued to serve as a basic denomination for paying the wages of the papal employees.

florette

A variety of the French **gros** struck under Charles VI of France from 1417 to 1422 with a value of 16 Tours **deniers** or 20 Paris deniers. The name means 'floweret' and refers to the three lilies, surmounted by a crown, on the obverse. There were later versions of the coin, including the copy of it made by Henry V in the Anglo-Gallic series in the early 15th century.

florin

The origins of the florin lie in the gold coins of Florence struck in the mid-13th century. On the *fiorino d'oro* ('gold florin') of 1252 the reverse bore a lily, or fleur-de-lis, which was the badge of Florence. This became very popular all over Europe, with the first English one struck under Edward III in 1344, and having a value of 6 **shillings**. The next appearance of the florin in England was as a silver coin, first minted in 1849 and assigned a value of one-tenth of a **sovereign**, as an initial move towards some kind of decimal system. The word 'florin' was dropped from the 2-shilling coin in 1937, and the name is now only rarely used for the 10-**pence** piece that superseded it after the introduction of decimalisation in 1971. The English name is based directly on the Italian *fiorino*, 'little flower' (i.e. the initial fleur-de-lis on the coin).

follaro

A copper coin of southern Italy struck from the 7th century and based on the **follis** (which see for the meaning of the name).

follis

The Latin word means 'money bag', and originally applied to a large leather purse used for holding army pay. By transference, the word then came to be used as a term for money of account, and finally, at the time of Diocletian's coinage reform of AD 296, as the name of an actual coin. It was designed to represent a double **denarius**, and was initially a silver-coated piece of copper. Some two hundred years later, the name was used for a large bronze coin issued under Anastasius, as part of his own currency reform. In this, 1 follis was worth 40 **nummi**.

forint

The Hungarian equivalent of the **florin**, today part of the country's monetary system and equal to 100 **filler**. As a modern coin, it was introduced in 1946 in place of the **pengo**. It bears two token 'flowerlets' on the reverse, although these are a poor imitation of the real thing on the original *fiorino d'oro*. (The Hungarian coin, too, is now an aluminium one.)

franc

The familiar coin and currency of France, first struck as a gold coin under Jean le Bon in the 14th century, and adopted as a basic denomination by a number of other countries, mainly French colonies. The coin itself, like many coins, has gradually been down-graded in value and appearance over the centuries, being issued as a silver coin in the 16th century and in more recent times as simply an aluminium piece. Its name almost certainly derives from the original Latin inscription on the coin, FRANCORUM REX, 'King of the Franks'. Apart from its use in former French colonies in Africa, the franc is today still the chief currency in Belgium, Switzerland and Luxembourg, among other European countries.

francescone

The silver **scudo** introduced into Tuscany in the second half of the 16th century by Francesco I and named after him.

franchi
The plural of **franco** (which see, below).

franciscus
A French silver coin worth 10 **deniers**, struck in the reign of Francis I (1515–47) and named after him.

franco (plural, **franchi**)
A silver coin of Lucca, Italy, struck in 1810 (although dated '1805–1807') and corresponding to the French **franc**, hence its name.

françois d'or
The name of the gold **pistole** of Lorraine struck under, and named after, Francis III, Duke of Lorraine (1729–37).

frederik d'or
A gold coin of Denmark, first struck under Frederick VI (1808–39). The coin was minted under succeeding monarchs, with the royal name duly altered on the obverse (as CHR. D'OR, for example, under Christian VIII, who came to the throne after Frederick), but with the coin name itself basically remaining the same. In the reign of Christian IX (1863–70) decimal currency was introduced, and the frederik d'or ceased to be struck.

friedenskreuzer
A 'peace **kreuzer**', or the name of a copper kreuzer of Baden struck to commemorate the Peace of Frankfurt (the final peace of the Franco-Prussian War) of 1871. The coin was inscribed in German: 'Zu des deutschen Reiches Friedensfeier 1871' ('To mark the German Empire Peace of 1871').

friedrich d'or
A gold coin of Prussia, struck in fairly large quantities as a type of **pistole** from 1740 to 1855 and named after Frederick the Great (Frederick II) in whose long reign (1740–86) it was first issued. See also **friedrich-wilhelms d'or** (below).

friedrich-franz d'or

The name of a gold coin of Mecklenburg-Schwerin, struck as a **pistole** under Grand Dukes Frederick Francis (Friedrich Franz) I (1785–1837) and Frederick Francis II (1842–83).

friedrich-wilhelms d'or

A gold coin of Prussia struck as a **pistole** under the three successive Kings of Prussia Frederick William (Friedrich Wilhelm) II (1786–97), III (1797–1840) and IV (1840–61). The name was usually shortened to **friedrich d'or**, however (compare this same name, above, for an earlier coin).

fu

The Chinese name used for copper **cash** from the earliest times. The word literally means 'water beetle', referring to the resemblance of the coins to this insect.

fugio cent

The first official coin struck in the United States, issued in 1787 as a copper **cent**. The reverse showed a sun dial and had the circular legend FUGIO 1787, with this Latin word meaning 'I flee', 'I hasten' and referring to the passage of time.

fun (fen) (plural, same)

The lowest value Chinese coin (usually spelt 'fen'), equal to one-hundredth of a **yuan**. The name, also used of a 19th-century Korean copper coin, means 'part'.

fünfer

A 'fiver', the colloquial German name for any coin with a value five times some established denomination, such as the 5-**heller** piece struck in Berne and other Swiss towns in the 14th century and the Swedish 5-**öre** coins struck in Riga and Pomerania after the Thirty Years' War during the Swedish occupation (1648–1720). The word is used today in modern Germany and German-speaking countries for similar multiples, such as the 5-**pfennig** coin.

fünfkreuzer
A 'five-**kreuzer**' coin struck with a value of one-twelfth of a **reichsguldiner** in 1559. It was abolished as early as 1566, however, since it could not be incorporated in the duodecimal system of 2-, 4-, 6- and 12-kreuzer coins. Despite this, it returned in 1753 as the result of the Convention that year establishing decimal values of 5-, 10- and 20-kreuzer coins.

fünfling
The 'little fiver', or 5-**pfennig** coin struck in about 1460, formally known as the **schildgroschen**.

fünfzehnkreuzer
The 'fifteen-**kreuzer**' coin of Austria struck in the Turkish War (1659–64) and introduced by Leopold I at that time to pay for military expenditure.

fürstengroschen
A type of **schildgroschen** struck under Frederick II, Elector (German *Kurfürst*) of Saxony (1428–64) together with his brother William III, Margrave of Thüringen. The coin became the model for the **groschen** struck subsequently by a number of German rulers.

fyrk
A silver coin of Sweden, worth a quarter of an **öre**, and struck from 1575 to 1601 (and as a copper coin from 1624 to 1660). The name is based on Swedish *fyre*, 'four'.

G

gabella
The name of a papal **grosso** struck in Bologna in the 16th century, and taking its name from the Italian word for 'tax', 'excise'. The 6-gabella coin was called *gabellone*, 'big gabella' and was equal to 4 **giulios**.

gazetta (gazzetta)
A small copper coin of Venice struck in the 16th century and having a value of 2 **soldi**. The name was a colloquial one, and is thought to be based on the Italian for 'magpie', *gaza*, with some allusion to the bird's propensity for stealing coins and other bright objects. More certainly, the coin name itself gave modern English 'gazette', which is the word for 'newspaper' in some languages. This was because early Venetian news-sheets cost one gazetta, either to purchase a copy or to hear the sheet read publicly.

genevoise
A colloquial name for the **écu d'argent**, value ten **décimes**, introduced in the decimal system of Geneva in 1794 (but abolished the following year). The coin replaced the earlier wording 'Genève République' by 'République Genevoise', hence the name. (It also replaced Latin 'Post tenebras lux' by French 'Après les ténèbres la lumière'.)

genovino
The standard gold coin of Genoa, struck in the late 13th century (although authorised over a hundred years earlier). The name is Italian for 'Genoese'.

george
The colloquial name of a number of coins bearing the head of a king George or a portrait of St George. These included the English **half-crown** of the 17th century and the **guinea** of the 18th, both of which portrayed the saint, and the 5-**dollar** gold coin issued in Canada in 1912, which bore the head of George V. See also the three entries below.

george d'or (georg d'or)
A gold coin of Hanover named after George III, under whom it was struck as a **pistole** in 1758 and 1803 and intermittently until 1857. From 1832 to this latter year the obverse bore the head of the King.

george noble
An English gold coin struck in 1526 under Henry VIII as a **noble** (with a value of 6 **shillings** and 8 **pence**). The name relates to the reverse, which showed St George slaying the Dragon. The piece was not struck after 1533.

georgtaler
The colloquial name of any **thaler** that bore a portrait of St George slaying the Dragon, in particular those of the 16th and 17th centuries, which were struck in several European countries, including England, Sweden, Russia and Italy.

gersh (guerche, guerch)
A silver coin of Ethiopia struck under Menelik II (1889–1913) with a value of one-tenth of a **talari**. The name is a version of **groschen**: compare **ghurush** (below) and also **kurush**.

ghurush
A large silver coin of the Ottoman Empire struck under Suleiman II in 1687 and having a name based on the **groschen**, although the piece itself more closely resembled a **thaler**. The coin was also frequently known as a **piastre**, especially in Europe.

gigliato

The name of a silver **grosso** first struck in Naples in about 1303 by Charles II of Anjou. The reverse of the coin bore a cross with lilies in its angles, and this is the origin of the name (from Italian *giglio*, 'lily').

giorgino

The name of an Italian **grosso** of the 16th to 18th centuries which bore a figure of St George. It was introduced in Ferrara by Alphonso II, Duke of Ferrara (1559–97) and in Modena by Duke Cesare (1597–1618).

giovannino

The name of a coin worth half a **grosso** struck in the Genoese Republic in about 1670. The piece bore a portrait of St John (Italian *Giovanni*), hence its name.

girasoli

A nickname for the silver coin with a value of 160 **sols** that was struck in Mantua, Italy, in 1629. The word is Italian for 'sunflower' and refers to the representation of this on the coin.

giulio

The name of a silver **grosso** struck under Pope Julius II (1503–13) with a value of 10 to the **ducat**. The name is the Italian version of the Pope's name, since his portrait appeared on the obverse. This was not the first issue of the coin, which had been in circulation since the 13th century, but it was the first to feature a papal portrait. Later the name was used of other papal pieces and Italian grossi.

giustina

A silver coin of Venice worth 10, 20 or 40 **soldi** and issued under Niccolò Trono, Doge of Venice, in the second half of the 15th century. The various denominations all bore a portrait of St Justina on the reverse, hence the name. Under Niccolò da Ponte, two larger types of giustina were introduced in the late 16th century: the *giustina maggiore* equal to 8 Venetian **lire**, or 160 soldi, and the *giustina minore*, with a value of 6 lire, 4 soldi (124 soldi).

glockentaler

A 'bell **thaler**', in a series of thalers issued under Augustus the Younger, Duke of Brunswick (Braunschweig), in 1643 to commemorate the liberation of the fortress of Wolfenbüttel on 13 November that year, during the Thirty Years' War. Seven types of this thaler are known, and they all bore on the reverse a picture of a bell or a bell tongue (or both).

gloriam regni

A colloquial name for a silver coin with a value of 5 or 15 **sols** struck in Paris in 1670 for use in French colonies in the United States. The name is the first two words of the Latin inscription on the coin: GLORIAM. REGNI. TVI. DICENT. ('They shall speak of the glory of thy kingdom', a biblical quotation from Psalm 145 : 11.)

glückstaler

A 'luck **thaler**', or one that bore a portrait of Fortuna, the Roman goddess of luck and happiness. There were several coins so named, including a commemorative piece of 1612 struck by the Duke of Mecklenburg-Schwerin, some Danish thalers issued later the same century by order of King Christian IV, and some mining coins (showing the source of the metal from which they were struck) of 1623 issued by Friedrich-Ulrich, Duke of Brunswick (Braunschweig).

goldgulden

The main gold coinage of southern Germany from the 15th century, issued as standard currency to supersede the gold coins of Italy, such as the **genovino** and **florin**, that had come to be widely used in the country a century earlier. The goldgulden were approximately the size of a **ducat**, but did not match its high standard of purity or weight, and they were in fact ousted in turn by it by the end of the 15th century. The name is really a tautology, since it means 'gold **gulden**', and 'gulden' itself means 'gold'.

gosler (**gösger**)

The original name of the one-**scherf** coin struck in the 16th century in the German city of Goslar. The name should not be confused with that of the **gosseler** (below).

gosseler

A silver coin of the Netherlands of the 16th century worth one-sixteenth of a **daalder**. The name of the coin was based on that of the **gosler** (see above), with which it should not be confused, however.

gourde

The French name for the **peso** when used as currency in French colonies in the West Indies in the late 18th and early 19th centuries, or for the coin that was physically cut from the peso in the form of a circle or a section, in proportion as one-fifth of the complete piece but in value one-quarter of it. (Such 'bits' of coins are technically known as 'cut money'.) The name is the French version of Spanish *gordo*, 'fat', 'thick', referring to the peso itself. The name remains today as that of the basic currency unit of Haiti, where the gourde is a silver coin divided into 100 **centimes**.

grain

The English name for the **grano** (see below) as the Maltese coin.

grano

Originally this was the name of a unit of weight (as 'grain' still is in many countries) of southern Italy. This was fixed as one six-hundredth of an ounce by Frederick II in 1222. Later, it was the name of the smallest copper coin in the coinage of Ferdinand II in Naples and Italy in the 15th century. Later still, the grano was the name of the smallest copper coin of Malta, with a value of one-third of a **farthing**. It ceased to be struck after 1899.

grazia (**crazia**)

The name of a base silver coin in several Italian states in the 16th century, probably originating in Florence. The name seems to derive from the inscription DEI GRATIA on the coin, although an early copper issue struck in Lodi actually had '1 GRAZIA' inscribed on it.

gregorina
A gold coin struck in Rome under Pope Gregory XVI (1821–46) and named after him. It had a value of 5 **scudi**. Compare **gregorio** (below).

gregorio
A silver coin struck at Bologna under Pope Gregory XIII in 1574, with a value of 1 **paolo**. Compare **gregorina** (above).

grenadino (granadino)
The name of the **peso** of Colombia in the mid-19th century, during the time when the country was known as New Granada. The coin itself was struck at Bogotá.

griffon
The name of gold and silver coins of the Netherlands that were struck in the 15th century with a representation of one or two griffons (the fabulous beast that was half eagle and half lion). The name applied really more to a type than an actual denomination, although some coins were inscribed in Latin: DENARIUS SIMPLEX NOMINATUS GRIFONUS ('A simple **denarius** called a griffon'). The most common coin to be so called was the silver **stuiver**. The device itself was a borrowing from Ancient Greek coins (e.g. the gold **stater**).

grivenka
The name is a diminutive of **grivna**, and originally applied to a Russian unit of weight used from the 14th to the 18th century for determining the weight of precious metals. There was no coin of the name as such.

grivennik
A Russian 10-**kopeck** coin, originally struck under Peter the Great as a silver piece in 1701. The coin continued to be struck regularly down to the 20th century, although from 1931 the metal used was a cupro-nickel alloy, not silver, and the name, based on that of the **grivna**,

became less frequently used. It is still current for this value, however.

grivenny
A colloquial name for the Russian copper 3-**kopeck** coin after the monetary reform of the 1840s, when it was worth roughly the same as a **grivennik**.

grivna
Originally a unit of weight in medieval Russia, then from the 11th century money of account, and finally a series of currency bars, gold from the 12th century and silver from the 13th, with the name subsequently used for the 10-**kopeck** coin that was more commonly called a **grivennik**. The name derives from the metal necklet (Russian *grivna*) worn by Russian women as an ornament in medieval times (as worn earlier by the Romans). As a currency unit, the grivna was superseded by the **rouble**.

groat
Today the name is popularly associated with the small silver English coin worth 4 **pence** as struck in the 19th century. Yet the name is much older than this and actually means 'great'! It derives from the Middle Low German *gros*, itself from Latin *grossus*, and in medieval times was used for all thick silver coins, as distinct from those that were thinner such as the **denier** and, especially, the **bracteate**. It really translated Latin *denarius grossus*, i.e. 'large **denarius**', and in English first applied to the 13th-century 4-penny coins introduced under Edward I as a copy of the French **gros tournois**. The coin itself was current until the 17th century. The 19th-century coin called 'groat' was a smaller version of it struck at the instance of the Member of Parliament Joseph Hume, and issued until 1855. In a general sense, the word was sometimes used for various low-value continental coins. Compare other 'great' coin names below, such as **groot**, **gros**, **groschen** and **grosso**.

groot
The silver **gros** of the Netherlands, based on the French **gros tournois** and first struck under John II, Duke of Brabant (1294–1312).

gros

A silver coin of France first struck in the 13th century with a value of 12 **deniers** and taking its name from the Italian **grosso**. The best-known type was the **gros tournois** (which see, below).

groschen

The chief silver coin of the Holy Roman Empire, taking its name from the French **gros**. The German word, meaning literally 'little gros', is still in use today as the name of the Austrian coin that is one-hundredth of the **schilling**, and in Germany generally still can be used to denote a 10-**pfennig** piece (now a copper or nickel coin). The name itself has a connotation of debasement, by contrast with the pure, fine **gros tournois**.

gröschlein (groschel)

A 'little **groschen**', or a coin worth a quarter of a gröschen struck as a German base silver piece from the 16th to the 18th century. The Silesian gröschlein of the 18th century had a value of one-and-a-third **kreuzers**. Earlier, in the 16th century, the half-**batzen** struck in southern Germany was also called a gröschlein.

grossetto

A 'little **grosso**', the Italian name of a half-grosso coin of the 15th century (although subsequently worth a whole grosso). In the late years of the century Augustino Barbadigo, Doge of Venice (1486–1501), struck a *grossetto a navigar*, or 'sailing grossetto', for the purposes of trading with the Middle East.

grosso

The Italian word means simply 'large', 'broad', and was first used of a silver coin struck in northern Italy at the end of the 12th century, the name itself implying a contrast with coins that were thinner and smaller (see **piccolo**). The grosso of Genoa had a value of 4 **denari**, although later issues, such as those of the Dukes of Milan, were worth 5 or even 8 **soldi**.

grossone

A 'big **grosso**', or the main silver coin of the popes at Rome from the 14th century to the 18th. The piece was a larger version of the standard grosso.

großpfennig

The original German name for multiple **pfennigs** or coins of similar type, such as the **gros tournois**, the **groschen** of Prague, and above all the Pomeranian **pfennig**, struck in 1395 in imitation of the **sechsling** of Lübeck. The name is a rendering of Latin *grossus denarius*, 'big **denarius**'.

gros tournois

A special type of **gros** struck at Tours, France, in the mid-13th century. It was a billon piece with a value of 4 **deniers** and on its obverse had a stylised representation of the Abbey of Tours. The coin was the model for many others, including the English **groat** and the Dutch **groot**, and was itself also known by several other names, including *denarius grossus*, *grossus turonensis* and *grossus albus*.

grosz

The name of the **groschen**, or a coin corresponding to it, in Slavic countries, in particular Poland, where it was first struck in imitation of the Czech grosz under Casimir the Great, King of Poland (1333–70).

groten

The name is an abbreviated form of German *Groten tournois*, i.e. **gros tournois**, and was given to a coin of this type that was struck in the 14th century with a value of 4 Meissen **pfennigs** (later, 5). The first Bremen groten was issued in about 1423, and from the 16th century to the 18th the coin was struck in large quantities.

guarani

The main monetary unit of Paraguay, divided into 100 **centimos**. The denomination was introduced in 1943 to replace the so-called '**peso** fuerte' (see **peso**). The name is that of the South American Indian language spoken in Paraguay, Guarani (one of the official languages together with Spanish). Paraguay is one of the few countries in the world that now no longer has any coins in its monetary system, and all its currency circulates in the form of banknotes, in value from 1 guarani to 10,000.

guerche (guerch) see **gersh**.

guilder
The English name of the Dutch **gulden**, used for the coin from about 1600, when it was first struck.

guinea
The well-known English gold coin, struck from 1663 to the end of the 18th century (but with a special issue in 1813). The name implies 'guinea-**pound**', since the original guineas were struck from gold brought to England from the Guinea Coast, in West Africa. It was thus initially an ordinary **sovereign** or 20-**shilling** piece, but from 1717 its value was fixed at 21 shillings. In more recent times it has been simply a money of account, and remained as a standard amount for a professional fee until the mid-20th century.

gulden
This was the name of the original gold coin of Germany, Austria, Hungary and other countries that corresponded to the **florin**, acquiring the name of **guilder** in the Netherlands and current from the 14th century to the 17th. The subsequent appearance of the silver **thaler** (as its equivalent) led to the name also applying to this coin, while the gold gulden was differentiated in German as the *Goldgulden*. (The silver gulden also became known as the **reichsguldiner**, which see.) The name 'gulden' itself simply means 'gold'. See also the next two entries below.

guldengroschen
A common German name in the 16th century for the **reichstaler** and the **reichsguldiner**, with the latter coin called by the name chiefly in Bavaria, Franconia and Swabia.

guldentympf
The name of the **gulden** struck in Poland from 1663 to 1665 and so called after Andreas Tympf (see **tympf**, its more common name).

gutergroschen
Literally a 'good **groschen**', and the name given from the end of the 16th century to the **fürstengroschen**. This had a value of one-twenty-fourth of a **thaler** by contrast with the **mariengroschen**, which was worth only one-thirty-sixth of a thaler. The name was in use to the mid-19th century.

gutfreitagsgröschel
A 'Good Friday **gröschlein**', otherwise a variant of the **dreier** that was a base silver coin of Silesia. It was struck in order to be distributed as alms to the poor on Good Friday.

gyllen
A Swedish name for the silver **gulden** first struck as a coronation piece by Gustavus Vasa in the first half of the 16th century and modelled on the contemporary German **guldengroschen**.

H

haidari (heidari)
A name for the double **rupee** of Mysore struck under the Sultan of Mysore in 1786, Tipu Sahib, and based on a surname (Haidar) of the first Imam.

halala
The smallest coin of Saudi Arabia, equal to one-hundredth of a **riyal**, with its name based on Arabic *ḥalāl*, 'lawful'.

halbskoter (halbschoter)
A coin struck in 1370 under Winrich de Kniprode, Grandmaster of the Teutonic Order, as a type of **groschen**. The piece was based on the **gigliato**, and, as its name indicates, had a nominal value of half a **scot**, i.e. 15 **pfennigs**.

haler
The smallest unit of Czech currency, equal to one-hundredth of a **koruna**. Its name is the Slavonic equivalent of **heller**.

half-cent
A small copper coin of the United States worth half a **cent** and struck from 1793 to 1857. It was never a popular coin (and even collectors spurn it today).

half-crown
The former familiar English coin, struck in every reign except that of William and Mary from Edward IV in the 15th century to Elizabeth II in the 20th. It was originally a gold coin, then (to 1946) a silver one, and finally (from 1949 until it was withdrawn from circulation in 1971) a

cupro-nickel piece. It consistently had the unchanged value of 2 **shillings** and 6 **pence**, that is, half a **crown** (which had a value of 5 shillings). The final issue was that of 1967.

half-dime
A silver coin of the United States with a value of 5 **cents** (or half a **dime**). It was first struck in 1792, then continuously (except for a suspension from 1806 to 1828) from 1794 to 1873.

half-dollar
A silver (now cupro-nickel-coated copper) coin of the United States with a value of 50 **cents**, or half a **dollar**. It was first issued in 1805.

half-eagle
A gold coin of the United States with a value of half an **eagle**, i.e. 5 **dollars**. It was struck from 1795 to 1916 and again in 1929. Like the eagle itself, it bore a representation of this bird on the reverse.

half-groat
A silver English coin with a value of 2 **pence** (half a **groat**), introduced in 1351, when the groat itself was first issued regularly, and current until the mid-17th century.

half-noble
A gold coin of England worth 3 **shillings** and 4 **pence** (half a **noble**), struck from 1344, under Edward III, to the time of Edward IV, in the 15th century.

halfpenny
The very first halfpennies, as individual round coins, were those issued in the 9th century by Saxon kings (especially Alfred) and by Viking invaders (mainly in East Anglia). However, the first literal 'half **penny**' was the one produced by physically cutting the early silver penny in two (compare **farthing**). There were round halfpennies again under Edward I in the late 13th century, and the familiar copper coin was first struck only in 1672, under Charles II. From 1860 the halfpenny was a bronze coin, like the penny itself and the farthing. The

100

last pre-decimal halfpennies were struck in 1967, and the first decimal ones in 1971. It ceased to be legal tender in 1985 and was finally withdrawn after its long life.

hardhead

A former billon coin of Scotland, also known as a **lion**. It was first struck in the mid-16th century under Mary, Queen of Scots, and had a value of 1½ **pence**. Its apparently obvious name is misleading, since it was actually a corruption of Old French *hardit*, that is, it derived from the same source as the coins known as **hardi d'argent** and **hardi d'or** (see both these below).

hardi d'argent

The 'silver *hardi*', or the Anglo-Gallic coin struck under Edward III in the 14th century and subsequently by kings of France. It had a value of 3 **deniers**, and derived its name from Philip III of France (1270–85), nicknamed *le Hardi* ('the Bold'). The coin was based on the French **masse d'or** that had been issued in his reign. Compare **hardi d'or** (below).

hardi d'or

The 'gold *hardi*', the equivalent of the **hardi d'argent** (see above) that was also struck under Edward III, and again subsequently under Richard II in the latter part of the 14th century and Henry IV in the early part of the 15th.

harp (harper)

The colloquial name for any Irish coin that had a prominent harp on the reverse, especially the **groat** and half-groat, struck from 1536 by Henry VIII, and certain 19th-century copper token pieces struck from 1820 under George IV.

harrington

The name of copper **farthing** token coins issued to supply low denominations for small change in 1613 by Lord John Harrington, who had been granted letters patent to do so. The issue ceased in 1643. (This was John Harrington or Harington, 1st Baron of Exton, who died in 1613.)

hatpiece
A gold coin issued under James VI of Scotland in 1591, with a value of 80 **shillings**. The coin bore a portrait of the King wearing a tall hat, hence the name.

heaume
The name of two French coins of the 14th and 15th centuries, respectively the gold *heaume d'or* and the silver *heaume d'argent* or *gros heaume*. The gold piece was struck under Louis de Mâle, Count of Flanders and Nevers (1346–84), and the silver by Charles VI of France (1380–1422). Both coins bore a representation of a helmet (French *heaume*), hence the name.

hecte
A gold or electrum coin of Ancient Greece with a value of one-sixth of a **stater**. The name relates to the denomination (Greek *hex*, 'six', *hektos*, 'sixth').

heller
A small silver coin first issued in Germany in the 13th century, although later debased and struck as a copper piece, with its currency spreading to Austria and Switzerland. Its name derives from the town where it was originally minted, Hall, in Swabia (today usually better known as Schwäbisch-Hall). The coin name, or a variant of it, still survives in the Czech **haler**, and in Austria the heller was current as one-hundredth of a **krone** from 1893 to 1925.

hemidrachm
An alternative name, meaning 'half-**drachma**', for the **triobol** of Ancient Greece.

hemihecte
A coin of Ancient Greece with a value of half a **hecte**, or one-twelfth of a **stater**.

hemiobol
A coin of Ancient Greece that had a value of half an **obol**, or one-twelfth of a **drachma**.

henri d'or
A gold coin of France first struck by Henry II in 1549 to replace the **écu d'or** (*au soleil*). It was the first French coin to bear a date.

hering (häring)
Literally a 'herring', as a colloquial name for the **dreier** of the early 16th century, circulating in large quantities in Swabia, and so named for the figures of two fishes on the Mömpelgard crest. This possession had passed to Ulrich, Duke of Württemberg (1498–1519), in 1503, and it was he who had issued the dreier shortly before this.

hessenalbus
A 'Hesse white' coin, or the name of a **groschen** first struck in the early 16th century in imitation of the Mainz groschen. From 1575 the coin bore on its reverse the inscription: ALBUS NOVUS HASSIAE ('new **albus** of Hesse'), and the actual name 'Hessenalbus' appeared on the coin from 1761. It was then worth 9 **pfennigs**. The hessenalbus ceased to be struck in the 19th century.

hexagram
A silver coin of Byzantium, introduced in the 7th century AD by Emperor Heraclius. Its name related to its weight, although in modern terms it weighs just *over* 6 grammes (but under 7).

holey dollar

The first coinage of New South Wales, Australia, also known as a 'ring **dollar**'. It consisted of a Spanish **peso** with its centre cut out (so that it was 'holey'), and with the resulting ring stamped FIVE SHILLINGS on one side and NEW SOUTH WALES 1813 on the other. The part cut out (a **dump**) was not wasted, but was in turn circulated as a piece worth FIFTEEN PENCE (reverse inscription). All the holey dollars were called in from 1822 and ceased to be legal currency in 1829. (Today there are very few left, and many collectors, especially Australians, avidly pursue them.) Similar coins were circulated in some other British colonies, such as Dominica, Trinidad and Tobago, in the West Indies, where the Spanish peso (or dollar) had also been current.

horngroschen

A silver **groschen** issued from 1465 to 1469 by Ernst and Albrecht, Dukes of Saxony, who ruled the duchy together with their mother Margarite and their uncle Wilhelm III of Thuringia. The coin was a groschen of the Meissen type, and on its reverse had a representation of a Thuringian helmet with the horns of an ox, hence the name.

horse and jockey

A nickname for the **sovereign** struck under George III (1760–1820), deriving somewhat irreverently from the figure of St George on horseback combating the Dragon, on the reverse of the piece.

hundesechstel

A 'dog sixth' coin, or the colloquial name for the Prussian coin with a value of one-sixth of a **thaler** that circulated in and around Berlin from 1822. The unusual name derives from the representation on the reverse of the piece of two links of a chain, half concealed by a crest or coat of arms. These fancifully resembled dogs, hence the name. Because of the misinterpretation, the two links appeared unobscured on mintings from 1823.

hyperper

A gold coin (the **solidus**) of Byzantium, current from the 6th century AD. The name means literally 'above fire' in Greek, denoting gold that was very pure, and that had been highly refined by fire. The coin name did not come into use until the 12th century, however.

I

ichebu (ichibu, itzebu)
A rectangular coin of Japan with a value of one **bu**, struck in the 19th century. The name, ultimately of Chinese origin, means literally 'one part', i.e. two words *iche*, 'one' and *bu*, 'part', 'division'. This refers to the fact that the coin was also worth one quarter of a **tael** (expressed in terms of a weight).

idra
A colloquial name for the **testone**, struck under Hercules I, Duke of Ferrara (1471–1505), referring to the figure of a hydra (Italian *idra*) on the reverse.

ikilik (ekilik)
A silver coin of the Ottoman Empire with a value of 2 **piastres** or 80 **paras**. The name derives from Turkish *iki*, 'two'.

imami
The name of a silver **rupee** of Mysore issued by the Sultan of Mysore, Tipu Sahib, in 1786 and honouring the Twelve Imams (the religious leaders of the Shi'ites, regarded as divinely inspired).

imperial
A name used for the gold 10-**rouble** coin of Russia first struck under Elizabeth I (Elizabeth Petrovna, Empress of Russia) in 1755. The coin was issued down to 1899, and there was also a **poluimperial** of half its value. The non-Russian name means what it says, describing the piece as an 'imperial' one (struck under an empress).

indio

A silver coin of Portugal struck for use in the Portuguese colonies under King Emanuel (Manuel I) in the 16th century. The name refers specifically to the Indian colonies.

interimstaler

A 'satirical' **thaler** struck in Magdeburg in 1549 as a jibe at the so called Augsburg Interim of the same year. This was a temporary doctrinal agreement between Roman Catholics and Protestants allowing Protestants to take communion in both kinds (bread and wine) and Protestant clergy to marry. On the original issues of the coin, the obverse bore the inscription PACKE DI. SATHAN. DV. INTERIM. ('Be gone, Satan, you Interim').

isabella

A colloquial name for a gold coin of Spain with a value of 100 **reals**, struck in 1864 under Queen Isabella II.

J

jacobus
The colloquial name for a gold **sovereign** struck under James I of England in 1603. The name was borrowed direct from the Latin version of 'James' on the coin, and jacobus was also used for the second issue of the coin the following year, when it was more formally known as a **unite**. By 1612 the unite was worth 22 **shillings**, and the sovereign 24.

jafari (jafri)
The name of a **rupee** or silver **fanam** of Mysore, struck under the Sultan of Mysore, Tipu Sahib, in 1786. It was named after the sixth Imam, Jafar Sadik.

jagdtaler
A silver **thaler** of Bohemia struck under Emperor Ferdinand II in 1626. The name, which literally means 'hunt thaler', refers to the portrayal of the Emperor on the reverse, where he is shown riding a hunting horse and accompanied by a huntsman and two hounds.

jakobstaler (jakobustaler)
A **thaler** struck in 1633 under Frederick-Ulrich (Friedrich-Ulrich), Duke of Brunswick (Braunschweig), and minted in silver from St James' mine at Lautental, in the Harz Mountains. (German *Jakob* is the equivalent of 'James'.) The coin bore a portrait of St James of Compostella. Coins like this that indicated the source of the metal from which they were minted are known as 'mining coins'.

jerome d'or (jeronimus d'or)
A name used for the **pistole** and half-pistole (worth respectively 10 and 5 **thalers**) struck in Brunswick (Braunschweig) from 1810 to 1813 by the King of Westphalia, Jérôme Bonaparte, younger brother of Napoleon.

jitney
A slang name for the United States 5-**cent** piece. The origin of the word is uncertain, but it could derive from French *jeton*, 'counter', 'token'. The term subsequently came to be used for a ramshackle bus, with reference to the standard fare on one of 5 cents.

joachimstaler

The original name of the **thaler** that was minted from silver obtained from the Joachimsthal mine. See the basic name for the complete story of this coin and the subsequent **dollar**.

joao
A gold coin of Portugal current from 1722 to 1835 and first struck under King João (John) V and having a value of half a **dobra** or 6400 **reis**. It became the main trading coin of the West Indies (see **joe**, below), and was widely imitated, in baser versions, by several countries, including America and England.

joe
The colloquial English name for the Portuguese **joao** (see above), in particular from its currency in the West Indies. The name should not be confused with that of the **joey** (see below).

joey
A colloquial name for the 4-**penny** piece, otherwise the **groat**, introduced in England in 1836 at the instance of the Member of Parliament Joseph Hume, and called after him. His intention was to issue a low-value coin for particular use when paying short cab fares, and the nickname almost certainly arose as a derisory one originally among cabmen themselves, who found they were offered the coin in place of the accustomed

sixpence. In the 20th century, the name was extended to the **threepence** (otherwise threepenny bit), especially in cockney usage. It was little heard by the time of the Second World War, however, and fell out of use altogether after it when the coin itself was withdrawn (1971).

judenkopfgroschen
Literally a 'Jew's head **groschen**', the colloquial name for a groschen of Meissen struck in the 15th century and depicting a Meissen helmet worn by a bearded head under a pointed cap. The name referred to a cap of this type that was frequently worn by Jews.

judenpfennig
The colloquial name of a copper **pfennig** in circulation in the Rhineland in the 1820s. The coins, which were current in abundant quantities, were largely imported or introduced to the province from elsewhere (including England, where some were minted in Birmingham), and were physically put into circulation by a well-developed network of money handlers and changers, amongst whom were a number of Jews. The coin became popularly associated with such dealers, and thus acquired its name.

justo
A gold coin of Portugal struck in 1485 under João (John) II and having a value of 2 **cruzados**. Its name comes from its inscription: JUSTUS ET PALMA FLOREBIT ('Justice and honour shall flourish').

K

kaisertaler

An Austrian **conventionstaler** (i.e. one struck according to the monetary convention of 1753 between Austria and Bavaria), with its name meaning 'imperial **thaler**', one that had been struck by order of the monarch.

kammerherrentaler

A colloquial name for the Prussian **thaler** of 1816 and 1817, with the circular inscription on the obverse: FR. WILH. III/K. V. PREUSS. This was short for 'Friedrich Wilhelm III/König von Preußen', i.e. 'Frederick-William III/King of Prussia'. The name of the coin, which literally means 'chamberlain thaler', is said to have arisen from the fact that when the King first saw it, he declared that he was not a 'Kammerherr von Preuss', i.e. a chamberlain named 'von Preuss', as the abbreviation K. V. PREUSS. could be taken. The story may well be apocryphal but it is certainly a fact that the particular piece was suddenly no longer struck, and that it was subsequently reissued with the circular inscription given in full, in an unabbreviated form. ('Chamberlain' is the usual English translation of German *Kammerherr*, but may suggest too lofty a title. In royal usage, a *Kammerherr* was an official in the personal service of a prince or sovereign, so a better equivalent in English might be 'gentleman of the bedchamber'.)

karbovanets

The Ukrainian name of the Russian **rouble**. The term arose in the 18th century, when for several years rouble pieces were issued that had oblique serrations on the rim instead of edge (milled) inscriptions. In Ukrainian, a serration is known as a *karb*, hence the name.

111

karl d'or

A gold German coin issued in 1726 by Charles Albert (Karl Albert), Elector of Bavaria, and named after him. The coin was based on the **louis d'or** and replaced the **max d'or**. It had a value of 10 **gulden**.

kas

The Danish equivalent of **cash**, and also the name of a copper coin struck for the Danish colony of Tranquebar, India, from 1667 to 1845.

katechismustaler

A 'catechism **thaler**', or the name of a range of thalers issued in the 17th century by Ernst (Ernest) I, Duke of Saxe-Gotha, with various religious quotations and verses, or with some kind of Christian symbolic depiction. The individual thalers had their own names, too, such as the *Glaubenstaler* ('Faith thaler') listing the attributes of God, the *Sterbetaler* ('Death thaler'), with a heart and skull as intimations of the apoplectic fits suffered by the Duke, an *Ehestandstaler* ('Marriage thaler'), showing a bride and groom, and relating specifically to the marriage of Prince Frederick in 1669, a *Tauftaler* ('Baptism thaler'), struck in 1670 to commemorate the christening of the Duke's first granddaughter, and a *Seligkeitstaler* ('Bliss thaler'), with quotations on the eternal bliss that the Christian faith promised.

katzengulden

A 'cat **gulden**', otherwise a half-derogatory, half-humorous name for the base **goldgulden** issued by Ludwig II, Count Palatine, in the first half of the 15th century. The 'cat' was the lion on the Palatinate coat of arms.

kazmi

The name of the coin with a value of one-sixteenth of a **rupee** or half a **fanam** issued by the Sultan of Mysore, Tipu Sahib, in 1786 and commemorating the seventh Imam, Musa Kazim.

kelchtaler

A 'chalice **thaler**', or the name of a thaler struck in Zürich in 1526 from silver church plate. Hence the name.

kinzigtaler

A **thaler** struck in the 18th century from silver extracted from the mine at Kinzigtal, which belonged to the Princes of Fürstenberg. This was thus a 'mining coin', since it bore the portrait of one of the princes on it. (There were various issues at different dates portraying different princes.)

kippergroschen

The name of a debased German **groschen** whose metal content was almost entirely copper. It was struck during the monetary crisis of the Thirty Years' War, and in 1620 it needed about 250 such thalers to have the value of one **reichstaler** (and as many as 420 in 1622). *Kipper* means 'clipper', i.e. someone who issues coins that are under the specified weight.

klappmützentaler

Literally a 'flat cap **thaler**', or the name of a **guldengroschen** of Saxony struck in some quantity in 1500 by Frederick the Wise, Elector of Saxony, together with Dukes Albrecht and Johannes or Johannes and Georg. Whenever these personages appeared on the coin, they were portrayed wearing a flat cap or hat (something like a priest's biretta), hence the name.

koban

A gold coin of Japan with a value of one-tenth of an **oban**, issued irregularly from 1591 to 1860. The name is Japanese for 'little division', 'small size' (as two words *ko* and *ban*), describing its relationship to the larger value oban.

kobo

A copper coin of Nigeria, introduced in 1973 and worth one-hundredth of a **naira**. The name is a native corruption of English 'copper', and was already in use for the **penny** that it superseded.

113

kolbenschilling

The name of a **schilling** struck by order of Gottfried IV Schenk von Limburg, Bishop of Würzburg (1443–55). The name means literally 'club schilling', and refers to the club that appears in the Bishop's family crest, with this in turn featuring on the coin.

kopeck (kopek, copeck)

The well-known small coin of Russia, originating as a silver piece first struck in 1534, when its weight was equal to that of the Novgorod **denga**. From 1535 it came to have a value of one-hundredth of a **rouble** (as it still has), and under the monetary reforms of Peter the Great it became a copper coin in 1704. The early kopecks bore a depiction of the tsar on horseback holding a lance in his hand. The Russian for 'lance' is *kop'yo*, and it was from this word that the name of the coin derived. The English version of the name is an attempt to represent Russian *kopeyka*. See also **novgorodka**.

korabelnik

The Russian name of the English **noble**, which depicted a ship (Russian *korabl'*) on its obverse.

korona

A silver coin of Hungary, current from 1892 to 1925, with its name meaning 'crown'.

koruna (plural, koruny)

A cupro-nickel coin of Czechoslovakia, first struck in 1922 and having a value of 100 **halers**. Its name means 'crown'.

kreuzer

Initially a silver German coin of the 13th century, the kreuzer later became a copper piece and was an Austrian copper coin worth one-hundredth of a **florin** down to the late 19th century. Its name means 'cross', and refers to the two diagonal (superimposed) crosses that were its distinguishing feature.

kreuzgroschen
A 'cross groschen', or a **groschen** of Meissen, struck under Frederick II, Elector of Saxony (1428–64). The coin bore a crest showing a lion with a little cross on each side, hence the name. (The crosses served to distinguish this denomination from the later **fürstengroschen**.)

kreuzthaler see **albertustaler**.

kriegsfünfer
A 'war fiver', or a popular name for the 5-**pfennig** piece struck by the German government in the First World War.

kriegssechstel
A 'war sixer', the colloquial name for a base coin worth one-sixth of a **thaler**, struck under Frederick II of Prussia (Frederick the Great) for trading requirements and military pay in the Seven Years' War (1756–63).

krona (plural, **kronor** [Swedish], **kronur** [Icelandic])
A silver coin of Sweden and Iceland, divided respectively into 100 **öre** and **aurar**. (The Swedish coin is sometimes referred to, even in numismatic literature, as **krone**, but should really be carefully distinguished from it today. Also, the Icelandic coin is properly spelt 'króna', plural 'krónur', which can in turn distinguish it from the Swedish coin, admittedly pedantically.) As with all similarly named coins, the reference is to a crown represented on one side or the other. Iceland adopted the denomination only as recently as 1925.

krone (plural, **kroner** [Danish, Norwegian], **kronen** [German])
The name of a silver coin of both Denmark and Norway, where it has the value of 100 **öre**, and formerly, of Austria, where it was current from 1892 to 1925 (with a value of 100 **hellers**). In the German Empire, too, there was a gold krone, with a value of 10 **marks**. As with the **krona** (above) and coins of like names, the basic reference is to the crown that appeared or appears still on them.

kronentaler

A 'crown **thaler**', or the name of a former coin of the Austrian Netherlands which in 1755 replaced the old **ducatone** of Brabant. The reverse of the coin was the same as that of the **albertustaler**, and thus showed a St Andrew's cross with three crowns. The latter gave the coin its name. The kronentaler ceased to be struck in 1857.

kroon

The basic monetary unit of Estonia from 1928 to 1940, being struck for general circulation as an aluminium bronze coin once only, in 1934. As with the two names above, the reference is to the crown that the piece bore.

krugerrand

The famous (or notorious) gold coin of South Africa, first minted in 1967 as a **rand** with a portrait of President Kruger, the former statesman and President of Transvaal (1883–1900), who died in 1904. The coin became a popular investment item in the 1970s, when it was smuggled into Britain. (The buying price for a krugerrand in 1967 was £16; in 1974 it was just under £100.)

kruisdaalder

A 'cross **daalder**', or the colloquial name of the daalder that was introduced in the Netherlands under Philip II of Spain in 1567. Its name relates to the cross of Burgundy that appeared on the obverse.

kurus

A small coin of Turkey otherwise called a **piastre** and having the value of one-hundredth of a **lira** (or Turkish **pound**). The name has been spelt in a variety of ways in the past, including *ghrush*, *ghurush*, *grouch*, *grush* and *gurush*, and these show more readily than the modern Turkish spelling (properly *kuruş*) that the original name was based on that of the **groschen**, **grosso**, and similar denominations. Although now a small coin, the kurus was current as a large silver piece as long ago as the 11th century.

kutb

A copper coin of Mysore with a value of $2\frac{1}{2}$ **cash** issued in 1792 by the Sultan of Mysore, Tipu Sahib, and with a name that is the Arabic for 'Pole Star'.

kwacha (plural, same)

A basic monetary unit and coin of Malawi and Zambia, with a value respectively of 100 **tambala** and **ngwee**. Zambia adopted the new decimal unit in 1968, and Malawi in 1971. In both cases the name is a native (Chibemba) one meaning 'dawn', that is, a symbolic 'dawn of freedom' for both countries. The word was already popular as a nationalist slogan, one chanted and shouted at rallies and meetings.

kwanza

The basic monetary unit and coin of Angola, with a value of 100 lweis. It was introduced in 1977 to replace the **escudo** (a legacy of the former Portuguese colony) and has a native (Bantu) name meaning 'first', 'beginning'. The word was already in use as the designation for an Afro-American cultural festival celebrated in the seven days before New Year's Day, when a new 'beginning' is awaited. The direct source of the name, however, is that of the river Kwanza (or Cuanza), one of Angola's longest, with this name therefore itself also meaning 'first', 'main'.

kwartnik

A former silver coin of Poland with a value of one-quarter of a **scot**. It was in circulation from the mid-14th century for about a hundred years, and has a name that describes its value ('quarter'). It was also known as a **polgrosz** ('half-**groschen**'), from its alternative value. When the kwartnik became debased in value at the end of the 14th century, too, and was worth only one-sixth of a groschen, it also became known as a **tretyak** ('three-er'). (See this entry separately for further detail.)

kyat

The basic monetary unit of Burma since 1952, replacing the **rupee** and having a value of 100 **pyas**. The name means 'weight', 'coin', and in origin corresponds, as the value of the coin did itself, to that of the **tical**.

117

L

lammdukaten (lämmleindukaten)
A 'lamb **ducat**', or a ducat of Nürnberg issued from 1700. The coin was designed to be given as a New Year gift, and the obverse portrayed the 'Lamb of God' (representing Christ) on the world's sphere. Hence the colloquial name.

lari
The name of a type of silver wire money issued in Persia in the 16th and 17th centuries, with the word later applying to a copper coin of the Maldive Islands, in the Indian Ocean, where it is still a current denomination, worth one-hundredth of a **rupee**. The name derives from that of the Persian province where the money first appeared, Laristan.

lat
A gold coin of Latvia, current from 1922 to 1941, and taking its name from that of the former Baltic State.

laubtaler
Literally a 'leaf **thaler**', with this a colloquial name for the silver German coin issued from 1726 to 1790 at a value of 6 **livres**. The reverse showed a shield with three lilies, framed by a laurel wreath, and this 'foliage' prompted the name. (The shield matched the French name of the coin as an **écu**.)

laurel
A colloquial name of the **unite** struck under James I (1603–25), referring to the portrait of the King showing him wearing a laurel wreath in place of the usual crown. See also **broad**.

119

laurentiusgulden

A 'Laurence **gulden**', or the name given to certain gold coins issued in Nürnberg from the 15th century to the 17th. These coins portrayed St Laurence and the gridiron on which he is traditionally said to have been martyred, and the name was taken from this.

leeuw

A gold coin of Brabant, Flanders and the United Provinces, issued under the Dutch warrior Anthony of Burgundy, Duke of Brabant, in 1409. The name is Dutch for 'lion', relating to the one that appeared on the obverse.

leeuwendaalder

A 'lion **daalder**', or a silver **thaler**-type coin first issued in the Netherlands in 1575. Like the **leeuw** (above), it showed a lion as a prominent feature (in this case one standing on its hind legs).

lek

The basic monetary unit of Albania, equal to 100 **qindarka**. Before 1925 Albania had no national currency of its own, and the coins that circulated were from various countries, including Italy, Greece, Australia and Turkey. In 1925 the **franc** was established as the national standard, and a lek was introduced to have a value of one-fifth of this. The name comes from the Albanian spelling of Alexander the Great (in abbreviated form). In 1947 the lek replaced the franc as the standard monetary unit. Alexander the Great was not only associated with this quarter of Europe (especially Macedonia), but was important in the history of coinage since he established several mints and was responsible for the great influence of Greek coinage in other areas of the world.

lempira

The basic monetary unit of Honduras since 1926, where it has a current value of 100 **centavos**. It is named after the Indian chief Lempira (1497–1537) who fought against the first Spanish colonists here. (The centavo still exists as a Spanish word, however, as does the name of the country itself.)

120

leone

1. A silver coin of Venice in the 17th century, with a value of 10 **lire**. The name is Italian for 'lion' and refers to the large one on the reverse.

2. The main monetary unit of Sierra Leone, divided into 100 **cents**. It was introduced in 1964 in place of the **pound**, and, obviously enough, takes its name from its country. There is no coin of the name (the highest denomination is the 50-cent piece), and the leone circulates in note form.

leopard

A gold coin worth half a **florin** struck, together with the florin, by Edward III in 1344. The obverse had a leopard bearing a banner, together with the arms of England and France. (The animal is actually a **lion**, but heraldically is a 'leopard' since this is the term for a lion with its head turned towards the viewer, otherwise a 'lion passant guardant', as in the Arms of England.)

leopold d'or

The name of the **pistole** struck under Leopold, Duke of Lorraine (1697–1729), and named after him. The gold piece was based on the French **louis d'or**.

leopoldino d'oro

A heavy gold coin struck in the first half of the 19th century under Leopold II, Grand Duke of Tuscany, and with a value of 80 silver **florins**. Its name is straightforwardly based on that of the Grand Duke.

leopoldo

A colloquial name for the **scudo** issued by the Grand Dukes of Tuscany Peter-Leopold (1765–90) and Leopold II (1824–59), relating to both of them. Compare **leopoldino d'oro** (above).

lepton (plural, **lepta**)

The name originated as that of a very small weight of Ancient Greece, and subsequently came to designate, in a general way, any small copper coin. In modern Greece, the lepton is still a small copper coin, but is now fixed as one-hundredth of a **drachma**. The Greek name simply means 'small'.

leu (plural, **lei**)

The chief monetary unit of Romania, introduced in 1867 as a gold coin equivalent to 1 French **franc**. From 1947, when the country became a people's republic, the leu acquired the value of 100 **bani**. The name means 'lion', from the heraldic beast on the original coin, but since 1947 it has been replaced by other, artisan symbols, such as tractors and lighthouses, and it is now minted from a cupro-nickel/aluminium alloy.

lev (plural, **leva**)

The main monetary unit and coin of Bulgaria since 1880, with a value of 100 **stotinki**. It was originally modelled on the French **franc** and bore a lion, hence its name. At first a silver coin, today, after devaluation, it is minted from a base metal. Compare the history of the **leu** (above).

liard

A small silver coin of France, first struck under Louis XI in the 15th century with a value of 3 **deniers**. In the mid-17th century, however, Louis XIV introduced a copper coin so named, worth a quarter of a **sol**. The liard, which was issued until 1793, and legal tender down to 1845, has a name that has been variously interpreted. The most probable origin is in a Gascon version, *li ardito*, of the name of the **hardi**, although some French etymologists derive the word from the name of the mintmaster who struck it, Guigues Liard.

libertina

A coin struck in Ragusa (now Dubrovnik, Yugoslavia) in 1791 and based on the **Maria Theresa thaler**. Originally the reverse showed the Ragusa coat of arms, but after the French Revolution in 1791, issues of the coin had a reverse bearing a crest in which there was simply LI/BER/TAS, written vertically in three syllables as the Latin for 'liberty', and this gave the coin its name.

libra

This was originally the ancient Roman weight equal to one **pound**. (This was not the same as the modern pound in weight, however, but equalled 327.45 g as compared to the avoirdupois pound which corresponds to 453.56 g. It was actually closer to the modern troy pound, as used for weighing precious stones and metals, which equals 373.24 g.) The Roman libra was the basis for all monetary dealings, and was thus equated with the **as** and was divided into 12 **ounces**. In early medieval times, the European libra, or its equivalent, was simply a money of account, with a value of 240 **deniers**. This therefore lay behind the pre-decimal English money system, with one pound divided into 240 **pence**. A reminder of this connection still exists in the form of the English pound sign (£), which is basically a letter 'L' (for 'libra') with a stroke through it to indicate a written contraction. (This can also be seen, or could until recently, in the symbol 'R$_x$' used by doctors and pharmacists to indicate a medical prescription, where it was a contraction for Latin *recipe*, 'take'.) Strangely, there has only been one actual coin named a libra, and this was a gold piece current in Peru from 1898 to 1930. Latin *libra* literally means 'balance', 'pair of scales' (compare Libra, the sign of the zodiac and its symbol).

lichttaler

A **reichstaler** struck under Julius, Duke of Brunswick (Braunschweig) from 1569 to 1587. The name derives from the representation on the obverse of a savage holding a treetrunk in his left hand and a lighted torch in his right (with German *Licht* meaning 'light'). The circular inscription on the coin was: ALIIS IN-SERVIENDO CONSUMOR ('I am used up in serving others').

liegnitzer

A colloquial name for the triple **groschen** of Silesia that was current in the 17th and 18th centuries. The name is that of the town and principality of Liegnitz (now Legnica in Poland).

ligurino

The name of a coin struck in Genoa in the 17th century with a value of 5 **sols**. The name refers to the head of Liguria on the coin: this was a personification of the ancient Italian region of Liguria which in its fullest form was the figure of a seated woman holding a lance in her right hand, with the left resting on the Genoese coat of arms. (A similar composition was the figure of Britannia on English coins.)

likuta (plural, **makuta**)

A basic currency unit and coin of Zaire, equal to one-hundredth of a **zaire**. The unit was introduced in 1967 (in what was then the Democratic Republic of the Congo), and the name is a native (Nupe) one, from *kuta*, 'stone' (having the concept of both a weight and a coin).

lilangeni (plural, **emalangeni**)

The basic monetary unit and coin of Swaziland, divided into 100 **cents** and introduced in 1974 to supersede the South African **rand**. The name is a native one from siSwati (a Bantu language), with *li-* the singular prefix (compare **likuta**, above), and *-langeni* from the root of the word for 'money'.

lion

The lion, as a royal beast, has long appeared on coins of many countries, from those of Ancient Greece to the present day. There have been several coins named after it, in different languages (see Appendix II, p.243 for some examples), and the best known English and French 'lions' (the word is identical in both languages) have included the following: (1) A silver **denier** of the Anglo-Gallic series, showing the Arms of Aquitaine, with a so called 'lion passant guardant' (otherwise a **leopard**, as the coin was alternatively known); (2) A gold coin of Scotland, first struck under Robert III (1390–1406), and issued to the end of the 16th century, when it became known as a lion noble; (3) A gold coin of France, often called a *lion d'or*, that was also known as a denier and that was struck under Philip VI of France in 1338 (the obverse portrayed the King with a royal sceptre and a lion); (4) The so called *lion heaumé*, or 'helmeted lion', issued by Louis de Mâle for Flanders in the second half of the 14th century (see **heaume**).

lira (plural, **lire**)
The basic monetary unit and coin of Italy and San Marino, divided into 100 **centesimi**. As the name shows, the origin of the currency was in the Roman **libra**, and the lira was long a money of account, not becoming an actual (silver) coin until about the 15th century. (One of the earliest issues was the coin that came to be called the **testone**.) The lira is also an alternative name for the Turkish **pound**.

lis
The name of two French denominations, respectively the *lis d'argent* and *lis d'or*, struck as a silver and a gold coin in the mid-17th century, both having a reverse showing a coat of arms surrounded by lilies (French *lis*), hence the name. The issue was only of brief duration, since the two coins failed to gain popularity against the already existing **louis d'argent** and **louis d'or**, which they respectively resembled.

litas (plural **litai**)
A basic monetary unit and silver coin of Lithuania from 1923 to 1940, issued at a level of one-tenth of a United States **dollar**, and divided into 100 **cents**. The name derives as a shortening of that of the former Baltic State.

litra
Originally a Sicilian unit of weight, corresponding to the Roman **libra**, the litra was first issued as a (silver) coin in the 6th century BC, when it was close in size and value to the **obol**. As both a silver and a bronze coin it was current down to the 2nd century BC. Its name (Greek for **pound**) comes from the same base as the libra itself, and ultimately gave modern 'litre' (or 'liter').

livornina
The name of a double **ducat** struck under Cosimo III, Duke of Tuscany (1670–1723). The reverse of the coin bore two rose bushes (hence its alternative name of

rosina) and the inscription LIBVRNI, 'of Livorno' (Leghorn). It was actually minted in Florence.

livre
The well-known French word for **pound**, originating from the Roman **libra**. Like the pound itself and the Italian **lira**, the livre was originally a money of account, with one livre equal to 12 **sols** or 240 **deniers**. (Impressively, this particular system, established by Charlemagne in the 9th century, persisted in Britain down to the latter half of the 20th century, with the initial letters of the three denominations recognisable as the old '£.s.d.'.) As a silver coin, the livre was also known subsequently as a lis d'argent. At the time of the French Revolution, at the end of the 18th century, the livre was superseded in coin money by the **franc**, although it continued as a money of account to the 19th century.

lorenzgulden
The name of a **gulden** of the local monetary system of Nürnberg, struck in 1429 with a reverse portraying St Laurence, hence the name.

lorraine

The name of the Scottish **testoon**, struck from 1558 to 1561. The name relates to the obverse, which depicted the crowned initials of Francis II and Mary Queen of Scots between two crosses of Lorraine. The currency of the coin was almost as brief as that of the royal marriage, which lasted only two years (from 1558 to the King's death in 1560, when he was still only sixteen).

louis d'argent
The silver coin of France that was introduced in 1641 under Louis XIII (hence the name) and that remained the standard coin of its type until the French Revolution at the end of the 18th century. Compare **louis d'or** (below).

louis d'or
The gold coin of France that was first struck under Louis XIII when the French coinage was reformed. It was modelled on the Spanish **pistole**, and indeed was

alternatively called this for some time. It ceased to be issued at the time of the French Revolution, at the end of the 18th century, and its effective equivalent, struck from the early 19th century, was the **napoleon d'or**. Its name obviously derives from Louis himself, and the following year it was 'paired' by the **louis d'argent** (see above).

lovetta
The name of a coin equal to half a **giulio** or 1 **grosso**, struck in Piacenza, Italy, under the Dutch Pope Adrian VI in 1522. The name (modern Italian *lupetta*) means 'little she-wolf', and refers to the representation of this animal on the reverse.

löwenpfennig
Literally a 'lion **pfennig**', and the name of a variety of **bracteate**, usually with a value of one-twelfth of a **groschen**, that was issued in Saxony and elsewhere in the early 15th century. The coin bore a shield with a heraldic 'lion rampant', hence the name.

ludwigsdor
The German name (as if 'ludwig d'or') for the **pistole** issued under the landgraves and grand dukes of Hessen-Darmstadt all named Ludwig, respectively Ludwig VIII (1739–68), IX (1768–90), X (1790–1830, being re-numbered I from 1806), and II (1830–48).

luigi
The Italian name for the **louis d'or**.

lushburg (lusshbourne)
The name of this coin is actually the anglicised name of Luxembourg, and it was a base issue made in imitation of the silver **penny** and imported from Luxembourg in the time of Edward III (1327–77).

M

mace

The mace originated as a Chinese unit of weight, equal to one-tenth of a **tael**, and subsequently became a money of account. The pre-revolutionary Chinese silver **dollar** was actually inscribed: 7 MACE 2 CANDAREEN, and as an individual coin the mace was a small gold piece circulating in Malay countries. The name derives from the Malay word for the coin, *mas*, itself from Sanskrit *maṣa*, 'bean', 'weight'.

macuquina

The name of an 8-**real** silver coin of Mexico, corresponding to the European **thaler** and first struck under Philip II of Spain in the second half of the 16th century. The coin was struck by hand on a roughly cut flan (blank piece of metal), and was of irregular shape, hence its name, which derives from Arabic *makuk*, 'wrong'. Coins of this type are generically known as 'cob money' (compare 'cobloaf' for a mis-shapen loaf).

macuta

The name of a Portuguese copper coin struck in the 18th century for Angola and other African colonies, when it had a value of 50 **reis**. The word is a native one deriving from Kimbundu *mukuta*, itself from Kongo *nkuta*. This literally means 'cloth', and originally applied to the pieces of cloth that circulated in these countries as money. Later, the name was used for money of account, and then finally was adopted by the Portuguese for the coin.

madonnina
The name of various Italian coins that bore a portrait of the Virgin Mary (the Madonna). The earliest such pieces were silver coins struck in Genoa in the 17th century. A much later madonnina was the papal copper coin with a value of 5 **baiocchi** struck in Rome in 1797.

magdalon (magdalon d'or)
A special type of gold **florin** struck in Provence in the second half of the 15th century under René I, Duke of Anjou. The name refers to the reverse, which bore a portrait of St Mary Magdalene holding a vase of oil.

magistertaler
The name of a **thaler** of Saxe-Weimar, struck in 1654 in honour of Prince Bernhard when he became head of the University of Jena.

mahbubia
The name of a silver **rupee** introduced in Hyderabad, India, in 1904 and named after Mahbub Ali Khan, Nizam of the Deccan.

maille (mail)
The name of the small base silver coin of France and Flanders, current from the 13th century to the 15th and usually having a value of half a **denier**, that is, an **obol**. The word was also used in a loose sense for money in general, especially when due to be paid at a particular time, such as a tax or rent. (This is the 'mail' of 'blackmail'.) Although linked in meaning, there are really two separate words here, with the coin name deriving from French *médaille*, 'medal', itself from Latin *metallum*, 'metal', and the generic word coming from Old Norse *mal*, 'speech', 'language', 'agreement'.

makuta
The plural of **likuta** (which see), with *ma-* the plural prefix.

mancus
The name of an Anglo-Saxon money of account from the 9th century, reckoned at 30 **pence** or one-eighth of a

pound. More specifically, it was also the name used in Europe for the Arab gold **dinar**, which was equal to 30 silver **deniers**. Either way, the name derives from Medieval Latin *mancusus* which itself was a borrowing from Arabic *manqush*, 'engraved'.

mantelet d'or
A 'gold mantlet', otherwise the name of a gold coin of France issued in the early 14th century by Philip IV. On the obverse, the King appears wearing a long fur cape ('mantlet'), and this is the origin of the name. The piece was also known as *petit royal d'or*.

maravedi
A gold coin struck in Spain by the Moors in the 11th and 12th centuries, and later used as the name of a very small copper coin circulating in Spain from the 16th century to the 19th, with a standard value of 34 maravedis to one **real**. The original piece was based on the gold Arab **dinar**, which had been struck under the Almoravid (Arabic *al-Murābiṭun*, 'the hermits') dynasty, and this gave the name. The coin was also known as a *marabotino*.

marcello
A Venetian silver coin worth half a **lira**, struck under the Doge of Venice, Niccolò Marcello (hence the name) in 1473. The name was sometimes used for coins of smaller fractions of a lira, such as one-fifth and one-eighth.

marengo
A gold coin of France with a value of 20 **francs**, struck in 1801 and 1802 to mark the French victory of the Battle of Marengo, in north-west Italy, in 1800.

margarethengroschen
The name of certain Meissen **schildgroschen** of the first half of the 15th century where the name of Margarethe, wife of Frederick II, Margrave of Meissen, appears on the coin together with that of her husband (or with that of her husband and of Frederick's co-ruler William III).

maria

A colloquial name for the Spanish silver coin with a value of 4 **reales** (or sometimes 8), struck by Charles II in the latter half of the 17th century. The reverse bore a large letter 'M' with an 'A' crossing it, a tribute to Charles's second wife Maria Anna of Bavaria-Neuburg, whom he married in 1689.

Maria Theresa thaler (Mariatheresientaler)

One of the best known and most widely dispersed silver **thalers** ever struck. The original coin of the name was the Austrian one of 1753, which bore a fine portrait of the empress Maria Theresa (1740–80). It continued to be struck after her death, but the date was 'frozen' at 1780. As such, the coin became increasingly popular and in demand for trading purposes, especially in the Middle East, where it was preferred over other types of thaler and respected for its high standard by comparison with modern debased coinage. It even continued to be struck in several countries down to the 20th century (such as at Vienna in the 1960s).

marienducat (mariendukaten)

A general name for any **ducats** bearing a portrait of the Virgin Mary. One of the earliest issues was a Hungarian ducat of the second half of the 15th century struck under Matthias Corvinus, King of Hungary. This showed Mary seated bare-headed on a cushion offering a fruit to the infant Jesus, whom she holds on her lap.

mariengroschen

The name of a **groschen** of Lower Saxony first struck in 1503 at Goslar and showing the Virgin Mary standing with the infant Jesus in her arms.

marienthaler

The name of any **thaler** that portrayed the Virgin Mary and infant Jesus, especially those struck in Hungary in the 17th century. The coin was also known as a *madonnentaler* (compare **madonnina**).

132

marigold
An obsolete English slang term for a **guinea**, referring to its colour. The name was current in the 17th century.

mark
The famous German monetary unit was originally a standard of precious metal, and this as established in Cologne in 1524 became accepted throughout central Europe. The first coin of the name was one struck in Lübeck in 1506. There was never an English coin called 'mark', although the term was used as a money of account, and in 1703, for example, Daniel Defoe was fined 200 marks. It was first struck as a silver piece in Germany as a standard denomination worth 100 **pfennigs** in 1873. The Old English name for the unit was *marc*, and this probably derived from a Scandinavian word that was ultimately related to Old English *mearc*, which was the other 'mark' meaning 'sign'. This could even have linked up with the physical 'marks' on the original metal bars.

markka (plural, **markkaa**)
The name of the Finnish equivalent to the **mark**. The coin was first struck in 1860 as a silver piece with a value of a quarter of a Russian **rouble**, since Finland was then part of the Russian Empire (from 1809 to 1917). It was itself divided, as it still is, into 100 **pennia**.

marti
A colloquial name for the Cuban gold 5-**peso** coin issued in 1915. The obverse of this showed the head of José Martí, the Cuban patriot (killed 1895, aged 42), hence the name.

masse d'or
The name is French for 'gold mace' (the sceptre, not the coin name), and the first coin so designated was the largest gold piece struck under Philip III in the late 13th century. It had a value of 25 or 30 Tours **sols**, and the obverse, which gave the coin its name, portrayed the King enthroned holding a sceptre.

masson
A billon coin of Lorraine struck in 1728 with a value of 2 **sols**, 10 **deniers**. The name was that of the mintmaster (Masson) responsible for producing the coins.

matapan
The first Italian coin of the **grosso** type, struck in Venice in the early 13th century under the Doge of Venice, Enrico Dandolo. The name is said to derive from that of Cape Matapan (now called Cape Taínaron), in southern Greece, since it was issued for the payment of troops on the Fourth Crusade (1204).

matthiasgroschen
A **groschen** struck at Goslar in 1410, bearing a portrait of St Matthew on its reverse. The coin, although increasingly debased, survived until the 18th century and was also known as a 'mattier' or 'matier', with one of the last issues actually bearing the former name in the inscription: 13 EINEN MATTIER, that is, '13 deniers to the mattier'.

max d'or (maxdor)
A gold coin of Bavaria struck in the 18th century under the Elector of Bavaria, Maximilian Emanuel, and named after him. It was worth 2 **goldgulden**, but had a short currency and in 1726 was replaced by the **karl d'or**.

mealha
The Portuguese name for the **maille**, with a value of half a **dinheiro**. The coin was struck under Alfonso II and Sancho II in the 12th century, and the name itself has the same origin as that of the maille.

medio
A former name of the Spanish half-**real**, as circulating in South America. The word is simply Spanish for 'middle', 'half', and although applied frequently to the half-real could also be used of other half-value coins, such as the *medio peso* or *medio corona*.

merk
A Scottish form of **mark**, with the name used of a silver coin first struck under James VI of Scotland (otherwise James I of England) in 1580. After the Union of Scotland and England in 1604 (see also **unite**), the merk was declared to have a value of 13½ **pence** when circulating in England. It was also known as the 'thistle half-**dollar**', from the thistle on its reverse. Charles II (1660–85) struck not only merks but half-merks and multiples of 2 and 4.

metical (plural, **meticai**)
The basic monetary unit and coin of Mozambique, divided into 100 **centavos**. The name is the Portuguese version of **miskal** (which see for the origin).

mezzanino
The name of the half-**grosso** first struck in Venice in the early 14th century under Francesco Dandolo, Doge of Venice. The name means 'half', derived from Italian *mezzo*.

mil
A small coin representing one-thousandth of a larger denomination, such as in Cyprus (one-thousandth of the Cyprus **pound**) and Malta (of the Maltese pound). The name derives ultimately from Latin *mille*, 'thousand', and can also be seen in other, non-monetary units, such as the mil that equals one-thousandth of an inch. Malta no longer has a 1-mil coin, since the value is too small. There is a 2-mil and 3-mil piece, however, with most coinage making up multiples of **cents**.

milan d'or (**milandor**)
Not a coin struck in Milan, but a Serbian gold piece with a value of 20 or 10 **dinars** (or **francs**) struck in Serbia (now a republic of Yugoslavia) in 1882 and bearing the head of the first King of Serbia, Milan.

milesimo
A low-value coin of Chile current from 1960 to 1975, worth one-thousandth of a Chilean **escudo**. The name is Spanish for 'thousandth' (compare **centesimo**).

miliarensis

A silver coin of Byzantium introduced by Constantine the Great and worth one-thousandth of a **pound** (of gold) or one-fourteenth (later, one-twelfth) of a **solidus**. The Latin name, itself based on *mille*, 'thousand', means 'containing a thousand'.

mill

A money of account in the United States, dating from the 18th century, with a value of one-thousandth of a **dollar**. The name, based on Latin *mille*, 'thousand' (or *millesimum*, 'thousandth'), was proposed by Thomas Jefferson (later President) in 1785, together with other coin names (see **dime**, **eagle** and, under **thaler**, **dollar**), and the nomenclature was made official in 1792. The name was also proposed in Britain in the late 19th century for the lowest coin in a projected new decimal system, when it would have replaced the **farthing**. The plan was never realised, however. (See also **victoria** in this connection.)

millieme

The lowest monetary unit and smallest coin of Egypt and Sudan, representing one-thousandth of a (respectively Egyptian and Sudanese) **pound**. Until 1971, there was also a millieme in the currency of Libya, when it was replaced by the **dirham**. The name is simply French for 'thousandth'.

millime

The lowest currency unit and smallest coin of Tunisia, equal to one-thousandth of a Tunisian **dinar**. The name is an Arabic version of French *millième*, 'thousandth' (see previous entry). The word is pronounced 'meleem' (rhyming with 'redeem').

milreis

A former monetary unit and coin of Portugal and Brazil, with a value, as its name implies, of 1000 **reis** or **reals** (see separately for the basic origin). The Portuguese milreis was the name used for the real when it became depreciated in the early 20th century, and it was used of a coin that was still officially designated a real. In 1911 it was superseded by the **escudo**. The milreis of Brazil also usually represented a real coin or its equivalent as a monetary unit, although one silver coin struck in 1922 was inscribed 2 MILREIS. In the monetary reform of 1942 it was replaced by the **cruzeiro**.

mina (plural, minae)

The original standard unit of weight and value in Babylonia and Assyria, later to be adopted by the Greeks as a money of account. The mina was divided into 60 **shekels**, while 60 minae were themselves worth 1 **talent**. In the Greek monetary system, a mina was worth 100 **drachmai**, while in the Persian system it was divided into 100 **sigloi**. The mina was not a monetary unit in the direct sense, but was simply a measure used for calculating large sums of money. The word derives from Greek *mna*, itself from Chaldean *manah*, 'to count', related to Phoenician *maneh*, 'weight'.

minuto

An Italian name for the **denaro piccolo** (see both these names separately), as circulating from the 13th century to the end of the 17th in a number of Italian states, especially in Genoa. The word is simply Italian for 'minute', 'very small'.

miskal (miscal, mithkal)

Basically, a unit of weight of various Muslim countries, for example Iran (Persia) where it equalled about 71 grains, and Turkey, where it was the equivalent of just over 74 grains. As a coin, it was a silver piece struck in Morocco in the late 18th century to correspond to the Spanish **piastre**, and in the monetary system introduced there in 1881 it had the value of a **real**. The miskal was also a monetary unit of Chinese Turkestan, and multiple values (2, 3, 4 and 5) were struck as silver coins from 1900 to 1911. The name utimately derives, through Turkish, Persian and Arabic, from colloquial Arabic *misqāl*, itself based on a root word meaning 'to weigh'. See also **metical**.

mite

The word has long been a general one to denote any small quantity, measure or object, including a variety of weights and coins, ranging from an old moneyer's weight equal to one-twentieth of a grain to a medieval money of account in England, equal to one-sixth of a **farthing**. There was also, of course, the biblical 'widow's mite', now generally believed to have been a **lepton**. The word is an Old English one, related to Middle Dutch *mite* which was itself the name of a copper coin and ultimately derived from Old High German *meizan*, 'to cut'.

mitre

The name of a base coin current in Ireland in the second half of the 13th century, so called from the representation of a bishop's mitre stamped on it.

mittelfriedrichsdor

The name of a gold coin of Prussia, struck under Frederick (Friedrich) II in the latter half of the 18th century during the Seven Years' War (1756–63). The coin was a 'medium' or 'intermediate' issue by comparison with the 'regular' **friedrichsdor**. Compare **mittelgroschen** (below).

mittelgroschen

A **groschen** struck in 1457 by Frederick II, Elector of Saxony, and based on the French **gros tournois**. Like the **mittelfriedrichsdor** (above) it was regarded as a 'middling' issue (German *Mittel*, 'middle', 'mean') by comparison with the standard groschen.

mocenigo

The name of a silver **lira** with a value of 20 **soldi**, struck in the second half of the 15th century under the Doge of Venice, Pietro Mocenigo (1474–5) and named after him. It was issued until 1575.

moco

A silver coin of the West Indies, cut from the centre of the Spanish **dollar** and issued as a piece in its own right. It circulated widely in Dominica and Guadeloupe in the 18th century and has a name that could perhaps derive from French *morceau*, 'piece', 'bit', since it in fact corresponded to the **bit**. On the other hand Spanish *moco* means 'slag' (waste material from smelting metal ore) and the derivation may better lie here.

mohur

The name of the standard gold coin of India, struck under the Mogul dynasty of the 16th century by various native princes, and later used as the name of the coin struck under British rule that was equal to 15 **rupees** and last issued at the end of the 19th century, when it was replaced by the **sovereign**. The origin of the word lies in Persian *muhr*, 'gold coin', 'seal ring', itself related to Sanskrit *mudrā*, 'seal', 'token'.

moidore

A large gold coin of Portugal current in the second half of the 17th century and first half of the 18th, when it also circulated in England, as did other continental coins. The first coin of the name was issued in 1575, with a value of 500 **reals**. The word is a contraction of Portuguese *moeda de ouro*, literally 'coin of gold'.

moskova

A name of the Moscow **denga** in use from the 16th century, and occurring in a number of commercial deeds of the time.

mouches

A colloquial name for certain issues of the **liard** (or 3-**denier** piece) issued in Avignon by Pope Urban VIII in the first half of the 17th century. The word is French for 'flies', referring to what was actually meant to be three bees on the coin. (For an even greater misattribution, see **mückenpfennig**, below.)

mousquetaire

The colloquial name of a 30-**denier** coin struck in French Canada in 1710. The name does not appear to relate to the inscription on the coin. Possibly it was issued to serve as wage-money for musketeers (French *mousquetaires*), or perhaps the many coins that were minted were regarded as 'invading' the country like musketeers.

mouton d'or

An alternative name for the **agnel**, literally a 'gold sheep'. The reference is to the figure of the Lamb of God with a banner ('Lamb and flag') on the obverse.

mückenpfennig

A colloquial name for the **pfennig** struck in 1696 under George William (Georg-Wilhelm), Duke of Brunswick-Zelle. The coin depicted a group of flowerbuds. These were not recognised as such, however, and were thought to be flies (German *Mücken*), hence the name. Compare **mouches** (above).

mungu (mongo)

A basic monetary unit and coin of Mongolia, equal to one-hundredth of a **tugrik**. The piece was introduced in 1926, and takes its name from that of the country and its inhabitants. (In Mongolian, the coin name is spelt *möngö*.)

münzgulden

The name of a monetary unit and coin of Lucerne, both current in the 18th century. The coin was issued in 1714 and had a value of half a **thaler** or 14 **batzen**. The name means simply 'coin **gulden**', 'minted gulden'.

murajola

A colloquial name in Italy for any billon coin with a dark colour (from Italian *moro*, 'dark'). The first such coins were papal issues of 1534 in Bologna and Piacenza, and in the 18th century the name particularly applied to multiple-value **baiocchi**.

mushtari

The name of a copper 40-**cash** coin of Mysore, issued in 1793 by the Sultan of Mysore, Tipu Sahib. The coin was originally called the **asmani**, but this was subsequently changed as Tipu had taken to naming the smaller copper coins by names of different stars. This coin, therefore, has a name that means 'Jupiter' (from the Arabic).

N

naira (plural, same)
The main monetary unit of Nigeria, divided into 100
kobo and introduced (in note form) instead of the
Nigerian **pound** in 1973. The name is based directly on
that of the country itself.

näpfchenheller
The name of a type of concave-shaped **heller** of uncertain
origin mentioned in official documents of Saxony from
1668 onwards, where it is referred to as a *Näpgen-Heller*,
with the first half of this a dialect German form of
modern *Näpfchen*, 'little bowl'. The coin may have been
a counterfeit one, or one that was minted illegally for
circulation in poor districts.

napoleon d'or
The well-known name of the French gold 20-**franc** piece
struck from 1803 to 1818 and bearing the head of either
Napoleon I or Napoleon III, and called after them. The
name also came to be used of any French gold 20-franc
coin, whether bearing the head of Napoleon or not.

navicella (navisella)
A colloquial name for the papal issue of the **ducat** that
was struck in Rome and Ancona in the 16th century. The
name is Italian for 'little boat', and refers to the reverse
of the coin, which showed a figure of St Peter in a boat.

naya paisa (plural, **naye paise**)
A unit of currency and coin equal to one-hundredth of a
rupee introduced in India in 1957. The name is simply
the Hindi for 'new **pice**', with the national wording

assumed on the adoption of a decimal currency in place of the anglicised spelling of the coin. See also **paisa**.

neugroschen

A billon **groschen** of Saxony struck in 1840. The coin was very similar to the Prussian **silbergroschen** (one-thirtieth of a **thaler**), but was not divided into 12 **pfennigs**, as it was, but into 10. The name is merely German for 'new groschen'.

neuner

A 'niner', or a name for various German coins that were either a ninefold multiple of a denomination or one-ninth of one. Examples are the one-ninth of a **thaler** that was struck in Nürnberg from 1622, or the copper 9-**pfennig** coin minted in Osnabrück.

neutaler

The Swiss name, meaning 'new **thaler**', of the French **laubtaler** worth 6 **livres**, and also of thalers struck in a number of cantons from 1796 with a value of 60 **batzen** or 4 old Swiss **francs**.

ngultrum

The main monetary unit of Bhutan, introduced in 1974 to replace the **rupee** but retaining parity with the Indian rupee. The ngultrum is divided into 100 **chetrums**, and has a name that is based on native (Tibetan-Burmese) *ngul*, 'silver', with *trum* a generic loanword for 'money', probably from Hindi.

ngwee (plural, same)

A basic monetary unit and coin of Zambia, introduced in 1968 to have a value of one-hundredth of a **kwacha**. The name, like that of the larger denomination, is a native (Chibemba) one, and also like it expresses an optimistic future for the country, since it means 'bright'.

nickel

The familiar name of the United States 5-**cent** piece relates directly to the metal, since regularly from the 19th century the coin has been minted from a cupro-nickel alloy (25% nickel and 75% copper).

noble

The English gold coin introduced in 1344 by Edward III at a value of 6 **shillings** and 8 **pence**, or one-third of a **pound** (or half a **mark**). As such it superseded the **florin**. Despite the fame of the coin, its name remains of somewhat uncertain origin. It does not appear to be a 'royal' name, like that of the **crown**, but is most likely to mean simply 'excellent' (compare **excelente**), and refer to the fineness of its gold. See also **rose noble** for a later type of noble.

nomisma

At first a Greek general term for money, from Greek *nomos*, 'custom', 'usage' (i.e. regarding money as something established by usage). Later, the word came to designate the scyphate (cup-shaped) gold coins of Byzantium, in particular the gold **solidus**. The basic Greek word here is the one behind 'numismatics', the study of coins. (The English term is a relatively modern one, dating mainly from only the 19th century, unlike the many subjects of its study.)

nonsunt

A colloquial name for the 12-**pence groat** issued under Mary, Queen of Scots in the mid-16th century, when she was married to Francis II of France (see **lorraine**). The name derives from the Latin inscription relating to this marriage: IAM NON SUNT DUO SED UNA CARO, 'Now they are not two but one flesh' (compare Genesis 2 : 24, Ephesians 5 : 31, and the marriage service in the Book of Common Prayer).

Northumberland shilling

A **shilling** specially struck in 1763 by order of George III for Hugh Percy, first Duke of Northumberland, when the latter was appointed Lord Lieutenant of Ireland. The coins were designed to be distributed in Dublin. Only two thousand were struck, with the result that today the coin is a great rarity among collectors.

novgorodka

A name for the **denga** struck in Novgorod in the 14th century, with a value equal to 2 dengi at Moscow (see also **moskovka**).

nummium (plural, **nummia**)

A unit of coinage of Byzantium, issued in the 1st century AD and equal to one-fortieth of a **follis**. There were only multiple coins (5, 10, 20 and 40), and the name itself derives, through Greek, from Latin *nummus*, 'coin'.

oban (obang)

A large, flat, oval-shaped gold coin of Japan (silver in some provinces) struck at intervals from 1573 to 1860 and originally, until devalued, worth 10 **kobans**. The name means 'great sheet', 'great division' (Japanese *ô-ban*), by comparison with the koban which was a 'little division'.

obol (obolus)

In Ancient Greece, the obol was both a weight and a small silver coin equal to one-sixth of a **drachma**. Later, in Roman times, it was a bronze piece. Later still, in early medieval times, the name (also spelt obole) came to be used for a small denomination in a number of European countries. In France, for example, it was worth half a **denier**, and in England corresponded to the **halfpenny**. It was also known as a **maille** (which see), especially in France and Flanders, and in Scandinavian countries, as well as Germany and the Netherlands, was similarly known as a **scherf**. The name itself derives, through Latin, from Greek *obolos*, literally 'nail', related to *obelus*, 'spit'. The ultimate reference is to the use of 'spits' or 'points' as both currency bars and for sacrificial purposes. (The name is also directly related to modern English 'obelisk'.)

octadrachm (octodrachm)

A silver coin of Ancient Greece having a value, as its name implies, of 8 **drachmai**. There was also a gold octadrachm issued under some of the Ptolemies, and this was alternatively known as a *mneion*, since it was worth 100 silver drachmai, otherwise a **mina** (which see, for the origin of the name).

145

octavo (ochavo)
The name of a copper coin of Mexico worth one-eighth of a **real**, struck from 1812 to 1863. There was also an earlier silver piece of the name, with the same value, issued under Ferdinand and Isabella in the late 15th century. For both coins, the name simply means 'eighth'.

octobol
A silver coin of Ancient Greece with a value, as indicated by its name, of 8 **obols** (or in real terms, one-third of an Athenian **tetradrachm** or four-sixths of a **drachma**).

oncia
The oncia was originally an Italian gold weight of the 10th century, deriving its name from the Roman **uncia**. In the 13th century one oncia was divided into 600 grains. In the 14th century it became a money of account in Florence, with 20 oncias equal to 1 **florin**. In the 18th century, the oncia was a gold coin struck at Palermo. For the origin of the name (and of English 'ounce') see **uncia**.

oncietta (onzetta)
A gold coin of Naples and Sicily, struck from 1818 to 1856 with a value of 3 silver **ducats**. The name is a diminutive of **oncia** (see previous entry).

onlik
A silver coin of Turkey in the 19th century, with a value of 10 **paras**, as its name indicates (from Turkish *on*, 'ten', and *lik*, 'times'). Compare **ikilik**, **altilik** and **yuzlik**.

onza
An alternative name for the gold coin worth 8 **escudos** of Spain and Latin America. The name is Spanish for 'ounce' (compare **oncia** and **uncia**).

öre (Danish and Norwegian **øre**) (plural, same)
The name was originally that of a small unit of weight in Scandinavian countries, equal to one-eighth of a **mark**. The first coin of the name was the Swedish öre struck in 1522 as a silver piece under Gustavus Vasa. Later, under the Scandinavian Monetary Union between Sweden,

Norway and Denmark, in 1872, the öre (or øre) was standardised as the one-hundredth of a **krona** or **krone**, as it still is today. The name of the coin derives from Latin *aureus*, 'gold coin' (see this separately as a coin name in its own right), but is surprisingly not connected with modern English 'ore' (as in 'iron ore'), even though this in turn derives from a Latin word (*aes*, *aeris*) meaning 'money' (basically 'bronze', 'copper', which is where the difference lies).

ort

The basic sense of the word is 'quarter' (German *Ort*), and this is often used to denote a quarter of a particular denomination, with the full form including this, such as **ortstaler** for the silver coin of the 16th to 18th centuries that was a quarter of a **thaler**. Some coins of this particular series were inscribed 1 HALB REICHSORT, showing the value to be half an ort in its own right (i.e. one-eighth of a thaler).

örtgen (oertjen)

This name is a diminutive of **ort** (see previous entry), so denotes a coin that has a value of a quarter of some denomination. The best-known piece was the billon and copper one issued in the Netherlands in the 16th century as a quarter of a **stuiver** (i.e. 2 **doits**). In the southern Netherlands the coin was also known as the **liard**, and in Prussia the piece was struck until 1752. The Dutch version of the name was *oertjen* (as in the heading above), although the last issue of the coin, in 1799 in Jever (Saxony), is usually referred to by its modern German name of *örtchen*.

örtli

A Swiss coin with a value of 4 **batzen** or a quarter of a **gulden**, which was in circulation from 1656 to 1811. The name means 'quarter', so the coin belongs to the same family as the **ort** and **örtgen** (above).

ortstaler see **ort**.

osella

A silver coin issued under the Doges of Venice from 1521 as a presentation piece. The osella was struck annually (to 1797) just before the New Year, when the gift would be made. The name is Italian for 'bird', 'wildfowl' (modern *uccello*), and arose from the fact that the coin replaced the seasonal New Year gift of wildfowl made by the Doges to the city councillors.

P

pa'anga
The main monetary unit of Tonga, introduced in 1967 to replace the Tongan **pound**. The choice and meaning of the name, and its preference over a proposed alternative, were explained in an article in *The Times* on 22 May 1966: 'Tonga has decided against calling its new decimal currency unit the dollar because the native word, "tola", also means a pig's snout, the soft end of a coconut, or, in vulgar language, a mouth. The new unit, to be introduced next year, will be called "pa'anga", which has only two alternative meanings – a coin-shaped seed and, not surprisingly, money.' The pa'anga currently circulates as both a coin and a note, and in value it is worth 100 **seniti**.

pagoda
The name of an ancient gold coin of southern India, struck in a large number of varieties from the 6th century down to the 19th, when it was superseded by the **rupee**. Early issues of the piece bore figures of animals, such as a lion, tiger, elephant or fish. On coins circulating from the 14th to the 17th century, portraits of Vishna or other Hindu deities appeared. But some issues showed a pagoda on the reverse, and this is the origin of the name.

pahlevi
A gold coin of Iran first issued in 1927 with a value of 20 **rials** (from 1932, 100 rials). It was named after Riza Shah Pahlavi (or Pahlevi), who came to power as shah (or king) of Iran (Persia) in 1925, and whose portrait appeared on the obverse.

paisa (plural, **paise**)

The native form, usually preferred today, for the Indian monetary unit that was formerly rendered in English as **pice**. In modern India, Pakistan and Nepal it is equal to one-hundredth of a **rupee**, and in Bangladesh one hundredth of a **taka**. (Under British rule in India, it was worth one-sixty-fourth of a rupee, or a quarter of an **anna**, or 3 **pies**.) When first introduced in India, in 1957 it was known for some time as a **naya paisa**. The word is a Hindi one, and probably derives ultimately from Sanskrit *pad*, *padī*, 'quarter'.

paolino

An alternative name for the **scudo d'or** struck by Pope Paul III in 1535. This bore a figure of St Paul, hence the name. (Compare **paolo**, below, for both its designation and origin.)

paolo

The name given to the papal **grosso** struck under Pope Paul III in the first half of the 16th century to replace the earlier **giulio**. The coin bore not only the papal crest but a figure of St Paul, and the name derives from him rather than the Pope (who nevertheless was associated with it and thus reinforced the name). Compare **paolino** (above).

papetto

A small silver papal coin with a value of one-fifth of a **scudo**, apparently first issued under Pope Benedict XIV in the mid-18th century, but in circulation till the time of Pius IX (1846–78). The name means 'little pope' (the diminutive relating to the size of the coin).

para

A copper or nickel (originally silver) coin of Turkey, now (since 1930) purely a monetary unit equal to one four-thousandths of a Turkish **lira**. It was first issued in 1623, but gradually depreciated until it was withdrawn altogether. The para still exists in Yugoslavia, however, where it is a coin worth one-hundredth of a **dinar**. The origin of the name is identical in both cases, since the word is simply Turkish (in turn from Persian) for 'piece', 'portion'.

pardao
A silver coin of the Portuguese colonies of Goa and Diu (India), current from 1570 to 1871 and better known as the **xeraphim** (although the name PARDAO appeared on it in the final years of its circulation). Its name derives, through Portuguese, from West Indian *partah*, itself ultimately from Sanskrit *prātāp*, 'splendour', 'majesty'. It is thus really a 'royal' name.

parisis d'or
A gold coin of France first struck under Philip VI in the latter half of the 14th century. The name of the piece refers to the fact that it was minted from the Paris **mark** (as a unit of weight of precious metal), which was heavier than the more common mark of Tours.

parruccone
The colloquial name, meaning 'big wig', for the **quadrupla** d'or of Spain, issued in the second half of the 18th century under Charles III. The name refers to the portrait of the King on the coin, where he is shown with thick curly hair.

pataca
The name of a monetary unit and coin of various countries at different times, mainly in Portuguese-speaking territory. It was originally the name of the Spanish **peso** in Brazil, and subsequently that of a silver coin issued for use in Portuguese colonies. Currently it is the main monetary unit and coin of Macau (formerly also of Timor). The origin of the name is disputed, but it is possible that it arose as a corruption of the Arabic name of the Spanish peso, which was *abu taka*, literally 'father of a gun', i.e. the 'name' of a coin (compare **abu midfa**). There were also related coin with similar names, such as *patacão* in Portuguese (literally 'big pataca') for a Brazilian coin of the 19th century worth 3 patacas, and the English alternative spelling *patacoon*, representing this.

patard
A silver coin of Flanders, Brabant and Burgundy, first issued at the end of the 15th century with a value of a

double **gros**. In effect the piece was a **stuiver** of the south Netherlands. The name was also used somewhat earlier for a French billon coin struck under Charles VI (1380–1422) with a value of 3 **deniers** (half a **liard**). The origin of the name is uncertain, but it could well derive from that of St Peter, since many patards bore a figure of crossed keys, the saint's emblem.

patrick
A small Irish coin current in the 17th century, when it was worth a **halfpenny**. The name is that of the patron saint of Ireland, who was portrayed on the piece.

paul d'or (pauldor)
The name of the **pistole** issued in the first half of the 19th century under Paul Frederick, Grand Duke of Mecklenburg-Schwerin, and named after him.

pavillon d'or
A gold coin of France introduced by Philip VI in 1339 as a **denier** piece. The obverse shows the King seated under an intricate canopy, 'pavilioned in splendour' as it were, and this (French *pavillon* meaning 'tent') gave the coin its name. The piece was also known simply as a **royal**.

peça (peza)
A gold coin of Portugal struck during the reign of John V in the first half of the 18th century as a half-**dobra** piece with a value of 4 **escudos** or 6400 **reals**. The name is simply Portuguese for 'piece'.

pegione (pigione)
A colloquial name for a silver coin of the **grosso** type, issued in Milan in the latter half of the 14th century under Galeazzo II and Bernabo Visconti, joint rulers as Lords of Milan. The obverse showed an eagle over a serpent, and the name seems to refer to this, with the heraldic bird mistaken for a dove (Italian *piccione*). Curiously (or deliberately), a later issue of the coin, under Massimiliano Sforza, Duke of Milan in the early 16th century, actually depicted a dove.

152

pengö
A silver coin of Hungary equal to 100 **filler**, current from
1925 to 1946. The name is Hungarian for 'ringing',
'sounding'. Compare **penny** (below).

penni (plural, **pennia**)
A copper coin of Finland, equal to one-hundredth of a
markka. The name is almost certainly a Finnish version
of German **pfennig** (probably in an earlier Low German
form *pennig*). See also **penny** (below).

penny (plural, **pence** [for sum of money, as 'ten pence'],
pennies [as individual coins])
The penny is the longest-lived English currency denomination. It originated as a small silver coin introduced
under Charlemagne to England in the 8th century, when
it was copied from the Roman *novus denarius* ('new
denier'). (Hence its abbreviation of 'd.' used until 1971,
when decimalisation took place, and the abbreviation for
the name became 'p.'.) The penny circulated not only in
England, but also in continental Europe in medieval
times, when it was one of the principal units of currency.
From the late 18th century, the coin was struck in copper
(as a **cartwheel**), and from 1860 it was reduced in size
and minted from bronze. From 1971, the decimal penny
became smaller still (and was officially known, and
inscribed, as 'new penny' for a time). Just as the Roman
denarius was equal to one two-hundred-and-fortieth of
the **libra**, so (until 1971) there were 240 pence in the
English **pound** (from 1971, 100). The name itself still
remains of uncertain origin, although the Old English
spelling of it (*pennig*) suggests a Germanic or Scandinavian
source, with the final *-ing* also seen in its multiple
(**shilling**) and fraction (**farthing**). It is possible the first
part of the name may relate to 'pan', and refer to the
shape of the original piece. Again, a connection with
pengö need not be completely ruled out, so that the coin
was simply a 'ringing piece'. See also **pfennig** (below).
Since decimalisation, the penny has come to be colloquially called a 'p', pronounced, and even sometimes
spelt, 'pee'. Even the **halfpenny** was frequently called a
'half a p', and the various multiples (2, 5, 10, 20, 50) are
usually known as a 'two-p piece', 'five-p piece', and so

on. In other words, the coins have no single name as the predecimal coinage had (**threepence**, **sixpence**, shilling, **half-crown**, and so on), nor are any colloquial names in use (such as the earlier **tanner** and **bob**). For a wider consideration of this negative naming aspect, see the Introduction, p.5.

pentadrachm

A silver coin of Ancient Greece with a value of 5 **drachmai**, as its name indicates. The piece must have been a rare one, since although it is mentioned in literature, none has actually been found. It is known, too, that a gold coin of the name was also struck under the Ptolemies.

peseta

The familiar unit of currency and coin of Spain, with a name that is a diminutive of *peso*, 'weight' and therefore of the **peso** (see below). The coin first appeared in the 18th century under the name *peseta provincial*, that is, as currency intended for internal circulation only in Spain. It was a silver minting, worth 2 **reales**. It became the standard monetary unit of the country in 1868, when it replaced the **escudo** as the main money of account. It is divided into 100 **centimos**.

pesewa

One of the two main currency units and coins of Ghana, 100 of which make a **cedi**. The name is a native (Fante) one, meaning 'penny'.

peso

The name is Spanish for 'weight', 'piece', and this is the famous '**piece of eight**' first struck as a silver coin in the 16th century with a value of 8 **reales**. More directly, the name relates to the fact that the original 'weights' or 'pieces' were cut from bars of silver brought back to Europe by the Spaniards from South America, in their early colonial ventures there, and subsequently used for minting coins. The name, too, is really a shortened form of Spanish *peso de a ocho*, 'piece of eight', further indicating its intended value. Today the peso is still the main currency unit and coin of many South and Central

American countries, divided into 100 **centavos**, including Argentina, Bolivia, Chile, Colombia, Cuba, Dominican Republic, Mexico and Uruguay. The so-called 'peso fuerte' (literally 'strong peso') was the name of the former main unit of currency in Paraguay, where it was superseded by the **guarani** in 1943. Similarly, it was the name of the gold peso introduced in Argentina in 1875 (although superseded by the **argentino** in 1881). The name denotes that this gold coin was 'strong' by comparison with the standard silver peso. References to the 'Spanish **dollar**' are also to the peso. Compare **peseta** (above), and see also **austral**.

petermännchen (petermenger)
A colloquial name for the **albus** (with a value of 8 **pfennigs**) struck at Trier during the Thirty Years' War (1618–48) and down to the end of the 17th century, by which time it had come to circulate widely in western Germany. The name means literally 'little man Peter', and referred to the portrait of St Peter on the coin.

pezzetta
A billon **grosso** piece of Monaco, struck from 1648 to the end of the 18th century. The name derives from Italian *pezzetto*, 'little bit', 'small piece', referring to the relatively small size and weight of the coin (although it was not small when compared to many other issues).

pfaffenfeindtaler
The name of a **thaler** struck in 1622 by the Duke of Brunswick (Braunschweig), Christian, as an anticlerical coin (i.e. an anticatholic one). The name derives from the inscription on the reverse, which was: GOTTES FREVNDT DER PFAFFEN FEINDT ('A friend of God is an enemy of priests'). The obverse showed an arm brandishing a sword and had the circular legend: TOUT AVEC DIEU.

pfennig
The well-known German coin originated in the early Middle Ages as a silver **denier**, later (from the 16th century) being issued as a copper piece, and eventually coming to have its modern value of one-hundredth of a

155

mark (in East Germany) or **deutschmark** (West Germany). The name derives from the same source, whatever it was, that gave the English **penny**, with both originating at about the same time in the 9th century. Like the penny, too, it was basically modelled on the Roman **denarius**.

philip (philippus)

The name of a gold **stater** of Ancient Greece, originally struck in the 4th century BC by Philip II of Macedon, and named after him. However, many much later coins also bore the name by reason of the fact that they were struck under a European ruler named Philip, or that they carried a depiction of St Philip (or both, with one reinforcing the other). A gold coin struck under Philip the Handsome (Philip I) of Spain (1494–1506), when earlier he was Duke of Burgundy, for example, had a portrait of the apostle Philip as a bearded man in a long robe carrying his attributes of a long cross and a book, and bearing the circular legend: S. PHILIPPE INTER-CEDE PRO NOBIS ('St Philip, pray for us'). The combination of royal name, saint's name, pictorial representation and inscription could hardly have produced any other name for the coin!

piastre

The denomination is familiar today as the standard monetary unit, usually 100 to the **pound**, in many Middle Eastern countries, such as Turkey, Egypt, Lebanon, Syria and Sudan, not always in coin form (except in multiples), since it is too small. It also came to be widely used as an alternative name throughout Europe and the Middle East for the Spanish **peso**, and certain Italian silver coins have also been called thus. The word came into English, via French, from Italian *piastra*, 'plate', where in turn it was a shortening of *piastra d'argento*, 'plate of silver', with this finally being a name for the Spanish peso as a silver coin. There have been some etymologists, however, who have claimed that the name actually derives from Italian *pilastro*, 'pillar', since the Spanish peso ('**piece of eight**'), intended for circulation in overseas possessions, had a reverse that depicted the

Pillars of Hercules (the two promontories at one end of the Straits of Gibraltar). This seems unlikely, however.

picayune
This was the name of the Spanish half-**real** piece when it formerly circulated in the United States, especially in Louisiana and other southern states. It was also an alternative name for the American half-**dime**. Originally, however, it was an old copper coin of Piedmont, when it was known in French as a *picaillon*. This in turn derived from Provençal *picaioun*, itself from *picaio*, 'money' (with an ultimate origin in *pica*, 'to strike', 'to prick'). The name went on to produce the standard English word 'picayune' meaning 'paltry', 'petty', 'small-minded'. (This word, however, is more common in American parlance than British, as is to be expected from the motherland of the coin itself.)

piccolo
The name of the Italian 'lesser' **denaro**, especially in the 14th and 15th centuries. It first appeared in Venice in the late 12th century, and came to acquire the alternative name of **bagattino**. The word itself is short for *denaro piccolo*, 'small denaro', by contrast with the standard denaro, and in particular this piece as the **grosso**.

pice (plural, same)
The older name in English for the Indian denomination today more usually called the **paisa**, especially before decimalisation in 1957, when it was worth one sixty-fourth of a **rupee**. The origin of the name is therefore identical to that of the **paisa** (which see).

picureddu
The colloquial name of the silver coin worth 20 **grani** issued for Naples and Sicily under Charles II in the second half of the 17th century. The unusual-looking word is a corruption of Italian *pecorella*, 'little sheep', referring to the representation on the coin of the Order of the Golden Fleece.

pie

The name of a former small denomination and coin of India, worth a quarter of an **anna** (from 1835, one-twelfth). The word is a native (Hindi) one deriving from Sanskrit *pādikā*, 'quarter', and the name is thus directly related to that of the **paisa**.

piece of eight

The popular English name of the Spanish **peso** (otherwise the **piastre** or 'Spanish **dollar**'), translating the full Spanish name *peso de a ocho*, itself relating to the value of the coin as a piece worth 8 **reales**. The name is usually thought of in the plural, and associated with hidden treasure, pirates and derring-do on the high seas. (It features prominently as a frequent utterance of Long John Silver's parrot in Robert Louis Stevenson's *Treasure Island*: 'Pieces of eight!')

pieter d'argent

A 'silver Peter', otherwise a type of **gros** of Brabant, struck in 1430 by Philip de Saint-Paul (as half the value) and by Philip the Good (as the full unit). The obverse of the coin bore a bust of St Peter, holding a book in one hand and a key in the other, and this was the origin of the name. Compare **pieter d'or** (below).

pieter d'or

A 'gold Peter', or the name of a gold coin of Brabant first issued in 1375 under Jeanne and Wenceslaus of Brabant, with a value of 4 Brabant **schillings**. The piece was named after St Peter, whose bust was portrayed on the obverse, where the saint is shown with a halo, holding a book in one hand and a key in the other. Compare **pieter d'argent** (above).

pistareen

A former Spanish 2-**real** coin of Spain, the West Indies and the United States, current until the 19th century. Its name is almost certainly a modification of **peseta**.

pistole

The well-known name originated as a French designation for the Spanish double **escudo**, a gold coin of the 16th and 17th centuries. Later, the name was transferred to the French **louis d'or** and similar coins circulating in a number of European countries, including Italy and Germany. In England, it was more usually known as the **doubloon**. Numerous German coins were struck in imitation of the pistole, and these are often known by the name of the reigning monarch at the time of issue, plus the suffix *d'or*, for example **georg d'or**, **karl d'or**, **max d'or**, **paul d'or**, **stanislaw d'or** and so on. The original Spanish coin continued in circulation down to the monetary reforms of Isabella II in 1847. The name of the pistole has still not been conclusively explained. Some maintain it is a shortening of French *pistolet*, literally 'little pistol', this obliquely referring to its small size by comparison with the French **crown** (i.e. the **écu**). (The coin, or the designation, was also known in English as 'pistolet', which seems to support this possibility.) Others, however, interpret the name as 'pistol' (the gun), but in a transferred sense to mean 'coin', much as 'écu' means literally 'shield' but figuratively 'coin'. (But this seems an unsupported theory.) Most likely, the name is an adaptation, influenced by *pistolet*, of Italian *piastra*, 'plate', in some kind of diminutive form. If this is so, the coin has a name that equates it in origin with that of the **piastre**.

plack

A Scottish billon coin, introduced in the second half of the 15th century under James III and struck until 1590. The name is a modification of French *plaque*, 'thin plate (of metal)', relating to the thinness of the piece. The plack usually had a value of 3 **pence** (occasionally 2 or 4).

plaquette

The name of a billon coin of the Austrian Netherlands and the bishopric of Liège (German: Lüttich), struck from 1755 to 1793 with a value of 14 **liards**. The word is French and means 'little plate' (compare **plack**, above), and the name was also used more generally for various square and polygonal (as distinct from round) commemorative and decorative medals from the time of the Renaissance.

plata provincial
Literally 'provincial silver', or the Spanish name for a silver coin issued under Philip V in 1716. The coin, which was worth 1 **real**, was struck with the aim of boosting the economy of the country, which had suffered as a result of the War of the Spanish Succession (1710–13), and it was thus designed for internal circulation only. Hence the 'provincial' part of the designation.

poisha
The basic currency unit and coinage of Bangladesh, equal to one-hundredth of a **taka**. The name is basically exactly the same as that of the **paisa**, which see for the origin.

polgrosz (polka)
The name of a coin worth half a **grosz**, struck under Ladislas Jagellon, King of Poland (1386–1434) and Casimir IV (1447–92). It remained the chief coin of Poland until the mid-16th century. The prefix *pol-* in Slavonic names (Polish, Russian etc.) means 'half'.

pollard
The name of an imitation or counterfeit base silver **penny** imported to England from the continent in the time of Edward I (1272–1307). Like the **crocard**, it was valued at 2 to the penny **sterling**, and was used as small change until it was prohibited in 1310. The name almost certainly refers to the head ('poll') on the coin, since many such pieces bore unusually stamped heads of monarchs.

polpolushka (polupolushka)
The name of a Russian copper coin worth one-eighth of a **kopeck**, struck under Peter the Great in 1700. The name means 'half a **polushka**', referring to the value of a quarter of a **kopeck** that the latter coin had after 1534.

poltina (poltinnik)
A Russian monetary unit of the 14th and 15th centuries, issued only in the form of bars with a value of half a **rouble**. From the second half of the 15th century to 1656 it was a money of account, worth 50 **kopecks** or 5 **grivny**.

160

The first actual coin of the name was the copper one struck in the second half of the 17th century under Tsar Alexis Mikhailovich, with a silver piece issued subsequently under Peter the Great. The coin continued to be struck down to the 19th century, only the actual name on the piece was replaced by the Russian value '50 KOPECKS'. The name reappeared, however, on Soviet coins in the 1920s, although it was not on the commemorative 50-kopeck piece issued in 1967 to mark the fiftieth anniversary of the October Revolution. The name derives from Russian *pol-*, 'half' and the old word *tin* meaning 'rouble', which itself derives from a verb meaning 'to cut' (see **rouble** for an identical origin). The variant *poltinnik* is still current in informal Russian to mean a 50-kopeck coin, or a sum of 50 kopecks.

poltorak (plural, **poltoraki**)
The name of a silver coin of Poland in the 17th century with a value of 3 **polgroszy** (or 1½ **groszy**). The coin, which was based on the **dreipölker**, has a name that is derived directly from the Polish for 'one and a half' (*poltora*).

poltura
The Hungarian name of the **dreipölker** or **poltorak** (see above), as struck in Hungary and Transylvania from the 16th century. The word itself is a modification of poltorak, and actually appeared on the coin.

poluimperial
A gold coin of Russia worth half an **imperial**, i.e. 5 **roubles**, and issued over the same period (1755–1899) as the larger denomination. The name has the familiar 'half' prefix (*pol-* or *polu-*).

polupoltina (**polupoltinnik**)
The name of a coin with a value of 25 **kopecks** (i.e. half a **poltina**), struck in Russia in the 18th and 19th centuries. (The original 'coins' of the name, however, were quarter pieces cut from the **thaler** in 1854, some years before the proper piece was first issued in 1701.) The name, as with all names of this type, denotes its value ('half a poltina').

polupolushka see **polpolushka**

polushka (poludenga)
A silver coin of Russia struck in the 15th century with a value of half a Moscow **denga** or a quarter of a Novgorod one (see also **moskovka** and **novgorodka**). After the monetary reform of 1534 the polushka had a value of a quarter of a **kopeck**. From 1700 to 1810 copper coins of the denomination were struck, with the name on the coin, but a subsequent issue, from 1839 to 1916, simply had the Russian for '¼ KOPECK'. The name is an Old Russian derivative of *polukha*, 'half', referring to its value (as reflected more obviously in its alternative name, 'poludenga').

pond
A gold coin of South Africa (more precisely, the Transvaal and Orange Free State, as they independently were then), current from 1899 to 1902 and equal to the English **sovereign**. The name is simply Afrikaans for 'pound'.

popolino
An Italian silver coin current from the 14th to the 17th century, initially with a value of 2 **soldi** (in Florence). The name actually means 'common people', 'populace', implying a coin that circulated widely and that was popular (in all senses of the word).

portugalöser
The name used in Germany for the **portuguez** and for coins based on it, especially in northern Germany, where they had a value of either 2½, 5, 10 (most commonly), or less commonly, 20 **ducats**. Most such imitations were issued in Hamburg from 1560, and later coins of the name were struck in Denmark, Poland and Sweden. The name relates directly to the portuguez itself.

portuguez
A large gold coin of Portugal with a value of 10 **cruzados**, struck from 1499 to 1557, when its successor was the **portugalöser** (above). The aim of the coin, as illustrated in its legend, was to promote Portuguese colonial policies

in India. Hence its name, which is simply Portuguese for 'Portuguese' (in today's spelling, *português*).

pound

The internationally known unit of currency, associated primarily with Britain, but existing in many other countries of the world as a standard denomination, such as Egypt, Sudan, Syria and, until 1980, Israel. The name derives from Latin *pondus*, 'weight' (as also reflected in such everyday words as 'ponder' and, in a less direct sense, 'depend'), and initially the Old English *pound* actually was a weight. In this manner, it originally corresponded to the **libra** of the Ancient Romans, which was also a weight before it was a coin. Moreover, the weight called 'pound', whether in England or elsewhere, was early equated with the libra, which explains why the abbreviation for the monetary unit in English is still '£', i.e. a letter 'L' as the initial of *libra* (while the abbreviation for the pound weight is still 'lb', an even more obvious derivation from the Roman name). As a weight, the English pound was the amount of silver that could be coined into 240 **pennies**, this particular figure based on the value of the **denarius** as one two-hundred-and-fortieth of a libra. The first coin to have this whole value (i.e. 240 pence or 20 **shillings**) was the **sovereign**, and although people spoke readily enough of a 'pound', the coin itself was rarely called by the name (which by the 19th century was associated more with the banknote for this denomination). Eventually, actual pound coins were struck in the 20th century (the first in 1983), and it was only really then that the name became properly and fully that of a coin. See also **decus** and **sterling**.

provinzialdaalder

A **daalder** coin of the Netherlands struck in various provinces and cities of the Netherlands from 1676, with a value of 5 **schillings** or 30 **stuivers**. The name, literally 'provincial daalder', refers to the many issues of the coin in the different provinces.

pruta (plural, prutot)

A main currency unit and coin of Israel from 1949 to 1960, worth one-thousandth of an Israeli **pound**. The name represents New Hebrew *pĕrūṭah*, from the Mishnaic Hebrew (the version of the language established in the 3rd century AD for the Jewish oral law) for **lepton**.

pskovka
A name for the Russian **denga** of Pskov or the Principality of Pskov from the 14th to the 16th century. Compare **moskovka** and **novgorodka**.

pu
The name of an early type of Chinese currency, with its name literally meaning 'cloth'. The coinage is said to be so called since by its shape it represented a piece of cloth from some garment such as a shirt or pair of trousers. If this is so, it resembled the earlier so called 'spade money', dating from the 7th century BC, which actually reproduced the shape of tools and implements of the era.

publica
A Neapolitan copper coin first struck in 1599 and current until the end of the 18th century. It initially had a value of 1 **tornese** (or **gros tournois**), although from 1622 this increased to 2 tornese and 3 from 1750. The name derives from the Latin inscription on the coin, either PUBLICA COMMODITAS, 'public comfort' (one hesitates to say 'public convenience', although this is more precise) or PUBLICA LAETITIA, 'public joy', 'public abundance'. ('Public' implies 'of the state'.)

puffin

The name of an unauthorised coin issued in bronze to equal a **penny** on the island of Lundy, England, with a corresponding half-puffin to match the English **halfpenny**. The coin was first struck in 1929, with the reverse showing a puffin (the name of Lundy actually means 'puffin island' in Old Norse, and the birds are a special feature there). The British government declared the coinage illegal, however, and they were soon withdrawn.

pul (pulo)
A Russian copper coin of the 15th century, current to the end of the 17th. Prior to this, it had been a coin in the currency of the khans of the Golden Horde, from the

13th century, and in much more recent times, the pul became, as it still is, one of the main currency units (although no longer a coin) of Afghanistan, where it equals one-hundredth of an **afghani**. The Russian name derives from an identical Turkish word meaning 'small coin', itself ultimately derived, through Greek, from Latin **follis** (which see).

pula

The main monetary unit of Botswana, introduced in 1976 to replace the South African **rand**, and divided into 100 **thebe**. The name is a native (Tswana) one meaning literally 'rain', and the word had long been used as a traditional salute or expression of good fortune and the like.

pumphosenkrone

A colloquial name in Germany for the Danish silver **krone** issued in 1655. The obverse of this showed King Frederick III wearing baggy trousers (German *Pumphosen*), hence the agreeable name.

punt

The main monetary unit of the Irish Republic, equivalent to a **pound sterling** until 1979, but now worth rather less. Despite the apparent gambling associations ('punters' who 'punt' on races), the name is simply the Irish version of 'pound', denoting both the coin and the weight. The Gaelic word appears on Irish banknotes. Like the English pound, the Irish punt is divided into 100 **pence** (Gaelic *pinginn*, 'penny').

pya

One of the main monetary (and weight) units of Burma, introduced as a currency denomination in 1952 with a value of one-hundredth of the **kyat**. The name is of the same origin as that of the **paisa** and **pie**, so ultimately derives from Sanskrit *pad*, 'quarter', here more loosely used of a coin that was a fraction of a higher denomination.

Q

qindar (qintar) (plural, qindarka)

The main monetary unit of Albania, introduced in 1947 and having a value of one-hundredth of a **lek**. The name indicates this denomination, since it derives from Albanian *qint*, 'hundred' (itself related to Latin *centum* and so to the coin name **cent**).

quadrans

The smallest Roman bronze coin in Imperial times, equal to a quarter of an **as**, with the name simply indicating this fraction.

quadrigatus

An alternative name for the Ancient Roman **didrachm**, current to the end of the second Punic War (202 BC). The silver piece showed Jupiter in a quadriga (a chariot drawn by four horses abreast), hence the name.

quadrupla

A large Italian gold coin current in the 16th and 17th centuries, having a value of 4 **scudi**, as its name intimates.

quart (quarto)

The name of various coins with a value of a quarter of some larger denomination, such as the French *quart d'écu* introduced by Henry III in 1578 with a value of 15 **sols**, and a coin of Gibraltar (originally a token piece called a 'quarto') issued in 1842 with a value of a quarter of a Spanish **real**. The name was also used to apply to the Spanish **cuarto**, where the value, however, was a multiple of four, not a fraction.

quartarolo
The Italian name, meaning 'quarter', of the billon coin struck under Enrico Dandolo, Doge of Venice, with a value of a quarter of a **denaro**. The denomination was current from the 13th century to the first quarter of the 14th.

quartens
The first large coin of Silesia, issued from 1292 to 1322. It had a value of a quarter of a **scotus** and was officially called a *denarius quartensis*, hence its name.

quarter
The straightforward name of the United States quarter-**dollar** (25-**cent**) piece, first issued in 1796. The name is equally familiar, too, for the Canadian equivalent, and it has even been sporadically recorded as an alternative for the English **farthing**.

quarter-eagle
A self-explanatory name for the United States former gold coin, first issued in 1796, that had a value of 2 **dollars**, 50 **cents**, with the 5-dollar multiple known as a 'half-eagle' and the 10-dollar coin the **eagle** itself. The piece was last struck in 1929.

quartillo
An English spelling of the name of the Spanish **cuartillo**.

quartinho
The name of the coin, first introduced in 1677, that had a value of a quarter of the Portuguese **moidore**. The meaning relates directly to the denomination, meaning simply 'quarter' (more exactly, 'little quarter', with the *-inho* suffix a diminutive, corresponding to the Italian *-ino*, as in the **quattrino**, below).

quarto
The name of both a billon coin of Italy worth a quarter of a **grosso** and current under the Dukes of Savoy from the 14th century to the 17th, and also of privately issued tokens of Gibraltar struck for two years from 1801.

Later, the latter were integrated into British coinage, and their name was modified to **quart** (which see).

quattie

A colloquial name in the West Indies for a coin (originally a small silver one) worth 1½ **pence**, i.e. a 'quarter' of a **sixpence**. The name and the coin (or its equivalent) were current in Jamaica in both the 19th and 20th centuries. Today, however, after decimalisation, the Jamaican **dollar** is divided into 100 **cents**.

quattrino

The name used formerly in various parts of Italy, including the Papal States, for the copper or billon coin that was worth a quarter of the **grosso**. The name means literally 'little quarter' (compare **quartinho**, above).

quetzal

The chief monetary unit (although no longer a coin) of Guatemala, comprising 100 **centavos**. It was originally a silver coin equal to one United States **dollar**, introduced in 1924. On both the obverse and the reverse was depicted the country's 'national' bird and emblem, the quetzal, hence its name (pronounced 'ketsel').

quid

The colloquial term for the English **pound sterling**, whether as note, coin or as an amount of money. (Unusually, the word does not add 's' in the plural, so that '£5' is said 'five quid'.) The term has been recorded as far back as the 17th century, and has also been applied in the past to the **sovereign** and **guinea**. The exact origin of the name is unknown. The obvious suggestion is Latin *quid*, 'what', used in a sort of oblique sense to mean 'something', 'wherewithal', and certainly 'quid' has been formerly current to mean 'thingness', 'what something is', especially in the phrase 'the quid of things'. Failing further evidence, one is obliged to leave the etymology there. The affectionate form 'quidlet' is still sometimes used.

quinarius

The name of a small silver coin of Ancient Rome, in both the Republican and Imperial periods, first issued in the 2nd century BC. Its name means 'containing five', and refers to its value of 5 **asses** (otherwise a half-**denarius**). The name was also used of the gold half-**aureus**, which represented 12½ silver denarii. Compare **quincussis** (below).

quincussis

Like the **quinarius** (above), this was also an Ancient Roman coin worth 5 **asses**. It was not a small silver piece, however, but a huge bronze one, weighing about 5 Roman **pounds** (**librae**), i.e. a massive minting of about 1.5 kilos, or over 3 modern pounds (3lbs)! The name is a mock-Latin one, based somewhat whimsically on *quinque*, 'five'.

quintina

A small silver coin of Naples current in the 15th century, with a value of one-fifth of a **carolino** (a type of Neapolitan **grosso**) or 12 **piccoli**. Its name relates directly to its value.

quinto

A silver coin of Florence in the 16th century, worth one-fifth of a **florin** (or 4 **grossi**).

quintuplo

The name of a gold coin of Naples worth 5 **ducats** as its 'multiple' name suggests.

quinzain d'or

The name of a coin projected by the Scottish financier John Law in his role as 'finance dictator' of France in the early 18th century. The name means 'gold fifteener', and presumably the piece would have been a 15-**franc** one. No trace of the actual coin has ever been found, however, even as a prototype or pattern.

quirino

A silver coin of Correggio, Italy, with a value of 5 **soldi** (or sometimes 8) with a portrait of St Quirinus on one side. The name is nothing to do with the 'five' root *quin-*, as many names above, but is thus the personal one, itself of disputed origin.

qursh
One of the three main currency units of Saudi Arabia, 20 of which make 4 **riyal**, and itself comprising 25 **halala**. This is the same name in origin as that of the **kurus** of Turkey, and therefore can ultimately be traced back (through Arabic *qirsh*) to the **groschen**, **grosso** and even the English **groat**.

R

rand
The chief monetary unit and coin of South Africa, introduced in 1961 in place of the South African **pound** with the adoption of a decimal currency. The rand is divided into 100 **cents**, and takes its name from the familiar abbreviation of the Witwatersrand, the important gold-mining region of the Transvaal. (This name itself is an Afrikaans one, meaning 'white waters ridge'.) See also **krugerrand**.

rappen
The name is still in use today in the German-speaking cantons of Switzerland for the **centime**. Originally, it was a small silver coin current from the 14th century as a billon piece worth 2 **deniers**. From 1799 its value was fixed at one-tenth of a **batzen**, or one-hundredth of a Swiss **franc**, as the centime is today. The name means 'crow', 'raven' (also 'black horse'), with colloquial and doubtless whimsical reference to the eagle on the first such coin, which was minted in dark silver.

real
The name of a Spanish, and subsequently also Portuguese, coin, first struck in the 14th century as a silver piece based on the French **gros tournois**. It remained the standard coin of Spain down to the 19th century, becoming established as one-eighth of a **peso** (hence the popular English name of the peso as a **piece of eight**). The Portuguese real became a copper coin by the 16th century, however, although multiples were still minted in silver. The latter became known in the plural as *reaes*, which later became *reis*. (The Spanish real, however, has a regular plural as *reales*.) Either way, the basic name

173

itself means 'royal', referring to the king who first struck it and whose portrait it bore. For the Spanish real, this was Pedro I (1350–69), who even had a crowned letter 'R' stamped on the coin. For the Portuguese piece, it was Alfonso V (1438–81). The latter coin was superseded by the **milreis** in the 17th century.

regensburger (ratisponenser)
The name of a type of **pfennig** struck jointly by Otto III, Duke of Bavaria, and Henry, Bishop of Regensburg, some time after 1290 in Regensburg (Ratisbon) itself. The coin was widely copied elsewhere in Germany throughout the next century, in various principalities and cities. The two names reflect respectively the German and Latin names of the city of Regensburg (Ratisbona).

reichsguldiner
An 'imperial **gulden**', or the name of a German silver **thaler** with a value of 60 **kreuzers** that was introduced as an equivalent of the **goldgulden** in 1559. The name properly relates to the reverse of the coin, which bore both the imperial German eagle and the imperial apple. The reichsguldiner circulated mainly in southern Germany.

reichsmark
The monetary unit of pre-war Hitlerite Germany, that in 1924 superseded the **rentenmark** and after the war became respectively the **deutschmark** in West Germany and the **mark** in East Germany. The *Reich* here relates of course to the Nazi dictatorship (the 'Third Reich').

reichstaler
The 'imperial **thaler**', issued in Germany from 1566 as a silver coin with a value of 68 **kreuzers**. It was in circulation until the 18th century, when it was superseded by the **conventionstaler**.

reinoldigroschen
The name of a coin with a value of 1 **groschen** (or the half or quarter of one), struck in the 15th century at Dortmund. The obverse bore a portrait of St Rainold, patron saint of Dortmund, and the circular legend on the coin ran: SANCTVS RAINOLDVS MARTIR –

MONETA NOVA TREMONIENSIS (the latter being the Latin name of Dortmund).

reinoldsgulden
The name of an ornate **goldgulden** issued by Reinold IV, Duke of Gelderland, in the early 15th century.

reis
The plural of the Portuguese **real**.

reisetaler
Literally a 'travel **thaler**', and the name of a Danish thaler (*kurantdaler*) with a value of 6 **marks**, struck on the occasion of visits by Danish kings or members of the royal family to Norway. Among such royal visitors, whose portrait and year of visit appeared on the respective issue, were Frederick IV (1704), Christian VI (1732–3), Frederick V (1749) and Christian VII (1788).

rempelheller
The colloquial (and mischievous) name of a **heller** struck in Wroclaw in 1422. This bore a portrait of St John, which according to some local wits bore a resemblance to an unpopular city councillor by the name of Rempel.

renminbi
The name for the currency and legal monetary tender of modern (Communist) China, the basic unit of which is the **yuan**. The name means literally 'people's currency' (or for a detailed breakdown *ren*, 'human', *min*, 'people', *bi*, 'currency'). The currency was introduced in 1948.

rentenmark
A monetary unit introduced in Germany in 1923 by the German Annuity Office (*Rentenbank*) to stabilise the currency. This is the **mark** that thus aimed to supersede the incredibly inflated values of existing marks, so that 1 rentenmark was worth 1 billion paper marks. The following year it was replaced by the **reichsmark**. See also **rentenpfennig** (below).

rentenpfennig

The **pfennig** issued at the same time as the **rentenmark** to stabilise the German currency. Coins with values of 1, 2, 5, 10 and 50 rentenpfennigs were struck, with the higher rentenmarks issued as banknotes.

républicain

A name current in Germany for the gold and silver coins issued by the first French republic under Napoleon as First Consul (1799–1804).

rial

The name of various coins of different countries at different times, from the gold coin of England worth 10 **shillings** struck under Edward IV in 1465 and the French gold coin struck by Philip IV and later monarchs that was current in Scotland and in the 15th and 16th centuries, to the modern rial as the standard monetary unit of Iran, Oman and certain other countries. (In Iran it is divided into 100 **dinars**, in Oman into 1000 **baizas**. It is also sometimes used as a currency name instead of the **riyal**, which see separately.) The earlier rial, the European one, almost certainly derived its name from the Spanish **real**, so means 'royal'. The Middle East rial, however, probably does actually relate directly to the riyal. The different coins are grouped together here, although today the preferred spelling for the English and Scottish coins mentioned above is the **ryal**, yet another variation on the royal theme. (And also see **riel**.)

rider

A former gold coin of Scotland, first struck under James III in 1475 and with an obverse that showed the king on horseback (i.e. as a 'rider') holding a sword. By about 1491 the value of the rider was 23 **shillings** and it continued to be issued under James IV (1488–1514). Compare **rijder** (below).

riel

The main monetary unit of Kampuchea (formerly Cambodia), introduced in 1955 in place of the Indo-Chinese **piastre**, and divided into 100 **sen**. The meaning

176

of the name is uncertain, but it is a Khmer word and not a 'royal' name such as that of the **real**, **rial** or **riyal**.

rigsbankdaler

The main monetary unit of Denmark from 1813 to 1875, with a value of half a **speciesdaler**, the previous currency. The rigsbankdaler (i.e. 'state bank **daler**') was divided into 6 **marks**, and each mark into 16 **rigsbankskillings**. The coin itself was a silver one.

rigsbankskilling

A historic monetary unit of Denmark, introduced in 1813 with a value of one ninety-sixth of a **rigsbankdaler** (see above). The higher multiples were silver coins (3, 4, 16 and 32), while the lower denominations were copper (2, 1½ and one-eighth). The main element of the name comes from the same origin as the English **shilling** and German **schilling**.

rijder

A gold coin of the Netherlands first issued in Gelderland in 1581, with a second issue two years later in Friesland. The name, which means 'rider', derives from the figure of a horseman on the reverse of the coin. Compare **rider** (above), where, however, the horseman was a particular monarch unlike the generalised Dutch rider.

rijksdaalder

The general name of various types of **daalder** issued in the United (Dutch) Provinces, such as the **arendsdaalder**, **leeuwendaalder** and others, with the name itself equating to the German **reichstaler** and so meaning 'state daalder'. (In some northern districts daalders were struck in imitation of the German coin.)

riksdaler

A name equivalent to the German **reichstaler** and Dutch **rijksdaalder** (above), so meaning 'state **daler**' in Sweden, where the first such denomination was probably the late 15th-century one under Sten Sture the Elder. The riksdaler in one form or another was current down to the latter half of the 19th century, when it was superseded by the **krone**.

ring dollar see **holey dollar**.

ringgit

The main monetary unit and coin of Malaysia, otherwise known as the Malaysian **dollar**, and divided into 100 **sen**. The name is a Malay word meaning 'jagged', 'serrated', referring to the milled edge of the coin, which in turn was based on the design and appearance of the Spanish **dollar** (the **peso** or **piece of eight**). 'Ringgit' was thus originally a nickname for the Spanish coin, or for any similar coin with a milled or floral edge.

rix dollar

The name of the Spanish **dollar** (**peso**) struck by the East India Company for Ceylon (now Sri Lanka) from 1803. The value of the coin fell from 3½ English **shillings** in 1809 to 2½ in 1814. In 1820 a new type of rix dollar was issued with a value of 1 shilling and 9 **pence**. The name itself is a part-copy, part-translation of the Dutch **rijksdaalder**.

riyal

Today the riyal is the main currency unit of Qatar, where it is divided into 100 **dirhams**, and Saudi Arabia, where it is equal to 20 **qursh** or 100 **halala**. (In both countries it is now a banknote, and there is no riyal coin.) The name is also used, confusingly, as an alternative spelling for the **rial**. The origin of the word is an Arabic borrowing (*riyal*), however, of **real**, as a general name for any large silver coin of Europe, such as the Spanish **peso** (or **piastre**) and the German **thaler** or its equivalent. See also **ryal**.

roda

The name of a Portuguese coin struck for the country's Indian colonies in the 16th century. At first an alloy coin (40% copper, 25% zinc, 32% nickel, 3% iron) it became an entirely copper coin from 1720, with a value of 2½ **reals**. The reverse had a representation of a Catherine wheel (i.e. the wheel on which St Catherine is said to have been martyred), and the name, which is simply Portuguese for 'wheel', relates to this.

rollbatzen

A type of Swiss **batz** struck in the 16th century as a silver coin. The name derives from the 3 rings on the coin, as part of the coat of arms of the local ruler under whom it was struck, Hugh of Hohenlandenberg, Bishop of Constance (Konstanz).

rosary

A base metal coin of the 13th century, imported to England from the continent at the same time as the **pollard**. It had the same value as the (silver) **penny**, and was current until declared illegal by Edward I at the end of the century. Its name refers to the rosette depicted on the reverse.

rose crown

The name used for the first milled **crown** issued under Charles II in the latter half of the 17th century. This had a figure of a rose under the bust of the King, with the addition said to indicate that the coin was struck from silver that came from mines in the West of England.

rosenobel

The name used in the Netherlands for the coin struck as a copy of the **rose noble** (see below).

rose noble

The **noble** as issued under Edward IV in the second half of the 15th century. This had a slight alteration on the standard coin, which was that the rose appeared (as a symbol of the house of York) on both the obverse and reverse, whereas on the noble it is only on the reverse. (The obverse rose, on the side of the ship in which the King is standing, is actually larger than the one in the centre of a radiate sun on the reverse.) The coin was also called the **rial** (or **ryal**). See also **noble** itself.

rose rial (rose ryal)

A gold **sovereign** of Scotland, first struck under James I in the early 17th century with a value of 30 **shillings**. The name relates to the reverse, which showed the royal coat of arms on a shield against a background of a large Tudor rose.

179

rosina

A colloquial name for the gold **florin** of Tuscany, struck in 1665 and 1718. The name relates to the two rose bushes depicted on the reverse.

rouble

The well known coin and currency of Russia and the Soviet Union, first struck as a silver denomination in the 17th century, and divided into 100 **kopecks**. The name relates to the portions ('cuttings') of silver bars that served as both a unit of weight and a currency in the 14th century, with the origin in the Russian verb *rubit'*, 'to cut', 'to chop'. As such, the rouble superseded the **grivna**. The ingenious theory that the coin name derives from Arabic *rubh*, 'quarter' (itself related to the name of the **rupee**), so that the rouble was worth this fraction of a grivna, is quite unsupported.

roverino

The colloquial name for the papal **florin** issued under Sixtus IV (1471–84) and Julius II (1503–13), referring to the coat of arms that the coin bore of the della Rovere family. (The real name of Pope Sixtus IV was Francesco della Rovere, and that of Julius II, Giuliano della Rovere.)

royal

An English name used fairly loosely for various 'royal' gold coins, such as the **real**, **rial** (or **ryal**, especially the **rose noble**) and so on. Robert Fabyan, the early 16th-century chronicler, recorded the appearance of the rose noble thus: 'This yere, was a newe coyne ordeyned by the Kynge, the whiche was namyd the royall, & was & yet is in value of .x. shillynges, the halfe royall .v. s.'.

royalin

The name of a currency unit of the former Danish colony of Tranquebar, southern India, from 1713 to the early 19th century. The name is a 'royal' one referring to the Danish royal arms on the coin, and was actually inscribed on the piece as 1 ROYALIN on the reverse.

rundstück

A 'round piece', or the German name of the Swedish *rundstyck*, a coin equal to the **öre** struck in the late 18th century, first as a silver piece, then as a copper one. From 1777 to 1818 the **riksdaler** equalled 48 **schillings** or 576 rundstück. The name is simply a distinguishing one for a coin in a series.

rupee

The name is best known as that of the principal monetary unit of India, struck originally as a silver coin in the 16th century (and still silver down to 1945), as well as the modern currency unit in several other Asian countries, such as Nepal, Pakistan, Sri Lanka and the Maldives. The larger countries have a rupee divided into 100 **paise**, but others have various smaller denominations, such as **cents** in Sri Lanka and **laris** in the Maldives. The name is often stated, even in numismatic works, to derive from a Sanskrit word such as *rupa* meaning 'cattle', much as the Roman word for 'money', *pecuniae*, related directly to Latin *pecus*, 'cattle'. In fact, however, the word, although deriving from Sanskrit, has its origin in *rūpya*, 'coined silver', in turn from *rūpa*, 'shape', 'beauty'. Furthermore, it is now considered most unlikely that there is any common link between the name of the rupee and that of the **rouble**, as was once proposed. Most modern dictionaries now give only the 'coined silver' origin.

rupiah

The main monetary unit and coin of Indonesia, divided into 100 **sen** and introduced in 1950. The origin of the name is exactly the same as that of the **rupee** (above).

rus

The proposed name of a new Russian monetary unit which it was planned to introduce in 1895 on the basis of the gold **rouble**. Patterns (prototype coins) were struck with values of 5, 10 and 15 rus (corresponding respectively to one-third of an **imperial**, two-thirds, and one imperial itself), but the coin was never issued. The name derives, obviously enough, from 'Russia', but more specifically from the Russian name of Ancient Russia, *Rus'* (sometimes known in English as 'Kievan Russia' or simply 'Russ').

ryal
The more common spelling today for the English and Scottish gold coins described under **rial** (which is still an alternative spelling, however).

ryo
A former monetary unit of Japan equal to the **koban**, so that the **oban** had a value of 10 ryos. The name is Japanese simply for 'part', and denoted a value rather than an actual coin.

S

salut d'or

A gold coin of France struck under Charles VI (1380–1422) and itself based on the Italian *saluto d'oro* issued under Charles I of Anjou for Naples some time near the close of the 13th century. An Anglo-Gallic coin of the same name was also minted by Henry V and Henry VI during the Hundred Years War (1337–1453). The obverse of these pieces showed the Archangel Gabriel appearing to the Virgin Mary (the Annunciation or, more precisely, Salutation of the Virgin), hence the name of the coin. In English the coin was often referred to as a 'salute'.

salute

The English name of the **salut d'or** (see above), especially one in the Anglo-Gallic series.

salvatortaler

A type of Swedish **thaler**, current from 1532 to 1653. The name refers to the reverse, which bore a figure of Christ with the circular legend: SALVATOR MUNDI ADIUVA NOS ('Saviour of the world, help us').

sampietrino

A copper papal coin with a value of 2½ **baiocchi**, struck from 1795 to 1799 at several mints in the Papal States under Pius VI. The obverse bore a head of St Peter, and this gave the coin its name.

sanese d'oro

The principal gold coin of Sienna, Italy, struck from 1340 as an equivalent to the **florin**. Its name means 'gold Siennese'.

san felipe
A silver coin of Portugal struck under Philip III in the first half of the 17th century for the Portuguese colony of Goa. The obverse bore a figure of a saint (intended to represent St Philip) in between the letters 'S.F.' (São Felipe). Hence the name of the coin.

san giovannino
A silver coin of Genoa issued in 1671 with a value of one-sixteenth of a **scudo**. The piece bore a figure of St John the Baptist, hence the name (actually a diminutive in the Italian).

san joao
A silver coin of Portugal struck under John IV in the mid-17th century for use in the Portuguese colonies of Damao and Goa. The obverse bore a figure of a saint with a banner (St John the Baptist) in between the letters 'S.I.', representing São João (St John).

san martino
A silver coin of Lucca, Italy, struck under Republican rule from 1660 to 1750, with a value of 15 **soldi**. The reverse had a representation of St Martin and the beggar (to whom he traditionally gave half his cloak). Lucca's cathedral is dedicated to St Martin.

san mauricio
A silver coin of Savoy, struck by Charles II, Duke of Savoy, in the first half of the 16th century. The name refers to the figure of St Maurice on horseback on the coin. There were two values: one issue of 9 **grossi** and one of 16.

sanpierino
An alternative name for the **sampietrino** or for any Italian coin bearing a figure of St Peter. All the papal pieces of the name were struck in Rome.

santa croce
A 'holy cross', or the name of a silver coin of Lucca struck in 1564 with a value of 25 **soldi**. The name describes the cross on the reverse and refers to the words there:

184

SALVATOR MUNDI ('Saviour of the world'). Compare the **salvatortaler** (above).

santims (plural, santimi)
The smallest unit of currency in Latvia from 1922 to 1940, equivalent to one-hundredth of a **lat**. The name, rather obviously, derives directly from French **centime**.

santo tomé (san thomé)
A gold coin of Portugal, struck in the mid-16th century for the Portuguese colonies in India, mainly Goa. The original issues had a figure of St Thomas on the obverse, hence the name. The initial value of the coin was 1500 **reis**.

san vincente (santo vincente)
A gold coin of Portugal first struck in 1556 and designed for her Indian colonies. The obverse bore a figure of a saint (St Vincent) holding a ship and a palm to represent Portuguese discoveries and colonial conquests.

sapèque
An alternative (French) name for the Indo-Chinese **dong**, deriving as a corruption of Malay *sa*, 'one' and *paku*, 'necklace', referring to the common method of stringing and carrying the coin. See also **sateleer**.

sarrazzino
A gold coin of the Crusaders based on the Arab **dinar**, having a name taken from that of the Saracens, who were Bedouin Arabs. It seems strange that the Crusaders, who were Christians, should have adopted a name derived from that of their Muslim enemies, especially as the coins specifically bore Christian inscriptions as 'propaganda' for their cause.

sateleer
An alternative name for the **dong** of Indo-China, with a derivation similar to that of the **sapèque**, from Malay *sa*, 'one', and *tali*, 'string', referring to the method of carrying the coins.

185

scalding
A Flemish coin introduced to England in the 13th century, and having a name with the same origin as that of the **escalin**, so relating directly to the **shilling**. In some texts of the 16th and 17th centuries, the coin is referred to as a 'stalding'.

sceat (skeat)
A small Anglo-Saxon coin, circulating mainly in southern England in the 7th and 8th centuries. It is believed to have been based on the Frankish **tremissis**. Its name, pronounced 'shat' by many numismatists as a close approximation of the original, is the Old English word meaning 'property', 'money'. A later debased form of the piece circulated in Northumbria, where it was known as a **styca**.

scellino
An alternative italianised form of the name of the **shilling** of Somalia, as the main monetary unit and coin in that country since 1962.

schaf (schaaf)
A colloquial name for the East Frisian double **stuiver**, first struck in the 16th century. The name is German for 'sheep', and is said to derive from a similar Dutch coin that bore the chain and order of the Golden Fleece, so that the schaf was probably based on this earlier issue.

schildgroschen
The name of a **groschen** of Meissen, struck in the mid-15th century. This bore the Landsberg (Bavaria) coat of arms on both sides, and gave the coin its name (with German *Schild* meaning 'shield').

schilling
Today the name is best known as that of the main monetary unit and coin of Austria (since 1925), divided into 100 **groschen**. In the past, the schilling has also been the name of various coins (originally usually silver, but later billon or even copper) of certain northern German states. Without detailing them all, it is enough to say that the name itself, wherever it occurred and is still found

186

today, is directly related to the English **shilling**, with both words gradually evolving from a blended (i.e. unified) original name.

schinderling

The colloquial name for a **pfennig** struck in Austria from 1457 to 1460, a period that came to be ironically known in German as the *Schinderlingszeit*, literally 'age of the fleecer', from the verb *schinden*, 'to fleece' (both literally and, as here, figuratively, in the sense 'extort', 'exploit'). Both names relate to the monetary policies of Frederick III, who being involved in a dispute regarding succession to the throne, as well as a money shortage, issued a pfennig in 1457 that had a virtually nil silver content, following it up shortly after with the minting of **kreuzers** that contained almost pure copper, instead of the expected silver. Austria subsequently lost much credit-ability for her silver coinage, now sadly debased.

schnieber

The name of a **groschen** struck under John Frederick (Johann Friedrich) the Magnanimous, Elector of Saxony, in 1534. The coin was minted at Schneeberg, hence the name (as a corruption of the original).

schockgroschen

The name of a **groschen** of Meissen and Prague that had a value of 60 to the **mark** in the 15th century when first struck. The name relates to the denomination, since German *Schock* means not only 'heap', 'mass' (to which is perhaps related the English 'shock' of hair) but also 'three score', 'sixty'.

schreckenberger

The name of a **groschen** of Saxony struck in 1498 out of silver from the mines at Schreckenberg and circulating widely (for example in the Netherlands). The coin was also known as an *Engelgroschen*, after the angel (German *Engel*) depicted on the obverse holding the electoral coat of arms.

schuppen

The name of a Frisian **pfennig** of the 11th or 12th centuries, given to it because of its shape and light weight, as German *Schuppe* means 'scale', 'flake'. The coin weighed less than 25 g. (i.e. about three-quarters of an ounce).

schüsselpfennig

The name of a small base silver coin struck in Germany in the Palatinate (Pfalz) in the 16th century and later copied in Brabant. The literal meaning is 'saucer **pfennig**', referring to the concave shape of the piece.

schwaren

A double-sided **pfennig** of Westphalia, so named in Bremen in the 14th century to distinguish it from the locally minted lighter **bracteate** pfennigs. The name means 'heavy' (modern German *schwer*), with this in turn based on Latin *gravis denarius* (as opposed to *levis denarius*, 'light **denarius**'), describing Roman coins.

schwarzburger

The name of a coin of the **pfennig** type current at the end of the 14th century, so designated after the mintowner, Gerard (Gerhardt) von Schwarzburg, Prince-Bishop of Würzburg (1372–1400). The coin was much copied at other mints.

schwertgroschen

The name of a **groschen** of Meissen struck from 1457 to the end of the 15th century as an imitation of the **schildgroschen**. The title means literally 'sword groschen', referring to the shield with crossed swords on the obverse, as the arms of the Electorate of Saxony. (Compare **schwerttaler**, below.)

schwerttaler

The name of a Bavarian **kronentaler** struck from 1809 by Maximilian I, King of Bavaria, and so called with reference to the crossed swords (German *Schwert*, 'sword') and sceptre under a crown on the obverse. Compare **schwertgroschen** (above).

scotus (scot)

The Latin name (appearing in more recent times as German *Scot*, *Skot*, *Schot* and so on) of a monetary unit with a value of one twenty-fourth of a German **mark**, or 30 **pfennigs**, widely current to equate to various standard coins of Prussia, Poland and Silesia in the 13th to 15th centuries. In Poland in the 14th century, for example, it was equal to 2 **groszy**. The scotus was originally purely a unit of weight, and although not a Roman denomination, seems to have been the name of a particular weight, or of a pair of scales for weighing coins. It is only doubtfully related to English 'scot' (as in 'scot-free' and 'scot and lot').

scudino

A gold coin of Modena equal to 103 **soldi** struck under Francesco d'Este, Duke of Ferrara (1629–58), and issued to the end of the 17th century. The name was used to distinguish this coin from the **scudo** di oro of 160 **soldi**, with the *-ino* ending a diminutive (as it were a 'little scudo', or at least a lesser one).

scudo (plural, scudi)

The name means 'shield', so that the Italian coin was the equivalent of the French **écu**. As the main silver coin of the country, it was the monetary equivalent of the German **thaler** and the English **crown**. The first scudo was struck in 1551 in Milan, with various other types following in different principalities and towns. However, there was a gold scudo (*scudo di oro*) that had first been struck even before this, in 1495, when it was issued by Charles VIII of France, as King of Sicily and Naples. In the Papal States the gold scudo was divided into 100 **baiocchi**, and elsewhere into 160 **soldi**. The silver scudo was also known as a **ducatone**. As the name indicates, the coin bore a shield (usually on the reverse) with a coat of arms or heraldic device. The Spanish equivalent was the **escudo**.

sebaldusgulden

The name of a **goldgulden** of Nürnberg struck in the early 15th century. Its reverse bore a portrait of St Sebaldus (see **sebaldustaler**, below).

sebaldustaler

The colloquial name of a **reichsguldiner** struck in Nürnberg in the 17th century. The reverse bore a portrait of St Sebaldus (Sebald or Siegbald) with the church dedicated to him. (This was Nürnberg's first church, the Sebaldkirche, built in the 13th century and formerly a place of pilgrimage. It still stands in the city as one of its oldest buildings.) Compare **sebaldusgulden** (above).

sechser

A 'sixer', or a general name for any German coin worth six times a basic denomination, which was often included in the full name, such as *Sechskreuzer*, *Sechsbätzner*, *Sechsgröscher* or *Sechspfennig*. In some parts of modern Germany (West or East) the name sechser was used until quite recently (perhaps still is, in places) for a 5-**pfennig** coin. Compare **sechsling** (below).

sechsling (sößling)

Like the **sechser** (above), a name that also means 'sixer', although this time more specifically for a billon coin of the early 15th century, struck in Lübeck, Hamburg and elsewhere, with a value of half a **schilling** or 6 **pfennigs**. The alternative name *sößling* was also used for identical coins issued in Denmark down to the 18th century.

sedicina

A coin struck at the Italian towns of Correggio, Urbino and Modena in the 16th and 17th centuries for trade with the Middle East. The piece was a copy of the Polish **trojak** and had a value of 16 **quattrini**, hence the name (from Italian *sedici*, 'sixteen').

seiseno

A copper coin with a value of 6 **deniers** struck in 1642 and 1643 in Catalonia, Spain, under Louis XIII of France. The name simply refers to its value, from Spanish *seis*, 'six'.

seizain

A coin worth one-sixteenth of a **thaler** struck at Geneva in 1624. Its name relates to its value, from French *seize*, 'sixteen'.

semis

A bronze coin of Ancient Rome worth half an **as**. Its name is a shortening of *semi-as*, denoting this value.

semprevivo

The name of a silver coin of Milan, with a value of either 5 or 10 **soldi**, issued in the first half of the 16th century by the Duke of Milan, Francesco Maria Sforza. Italian *semprevivo* is the name of the plant known as the house leek (*Sempervivum tectorum*), and this is seen on the coin apparently sprouting from three hillocks.

semuncia

An early bronze coin of Ancient Rome worth half an **uncia**. As its name suggests, it was originally a weight of half an ounce (i.e. *semi-uncia*).

sen

Originally the main copper coin of Japan, introduced in the 8th century in imitation of the Chinese **cash**, the sen exists today as the chief minor currency of certain eastern countries such as Indonesia (where it is worth one-hundredth of a **rupiah**) and, from 1954, Kampuchea (Cambodia), as the same fraction of a **riel**. In Brunei, too, it is one-hundredth of the Brunei **dollar**. The name itself is also ultimately from the Chinese, where *ch'ien* means simply 'coin'. In some countries it seems to have blended with **cent**, as formerly in Malaysia, where both names were used to denote the coin that was one-hundredth of the Malaysian dollar (or **ringgit**). This is simply a coincidence, however, since the two names are of quite different origin, respectively eastern and western. But compare **sene** and **seniti** (below), and see also **tsien**.

sene

The standard minor currency and coin of Western Samoa, equal to one-hundredth of a **tala**. Like this other name, sene is a corruption of English, in this case **cent** (no doubt via Polynesian). Compare also the **seniti** (below).

sengi (plural, same)

The smallest main monetary unit of Zaire, equal to one-hundredth of a **likuta** or one ten-thousandth of a **zaire**. The name is a native one, that of the Senga (Nsenga) people who originated from what is now Zaire, but who today have settled in the Zambezi River area of eastern Zambia. The unit was introduced in 1967 and there is now only a 10-sengi coin as the lowest denomination.

seniti

The lowest monetary unit and coin of Tonga, equal to one-hundredth of a **pa'anga**. As for the **sene** (above), the name is a modification of English **cent**.

sent

A monetary unit and coin of Estonia from 1928 to 1940, equal to one-hundredth of a **kroon**. The name is an obvious version of **cent**, probably coming immediately from Finnish *sentti*.

sequin

The English corruption of the name of the Italian **zecchino**, and for equivalent gold coins of the Turkish (Ottoman) Empire. The word came into English via the French, and itself went on to give the standard word 'sequin' meaning 'ornamental shining disc on clothing'. Another name for the same coin was **seraph** (see below).

seraph

An alternative name for the **sequin** (see above), otherwise the **zecchino**. This time the corruption came direct from Arabic *sharif*, literally 'illustrious', possibly influenced, at any rate in spelling, by 'seraphim' (but not by 'seraph' which is first recorded later than the coin name). Compare however **seraphin** (below), and also **ashrafi**.

seraphin

An English corruption of the name of the Portuguese **xeraphim** (itself a corruption of the same origin that gave the name of the **seraph**, above).

sesino
The name of a copper coin of Italy in the 18th century which had a value of 6 **denari** or half a **soldo**. Its name derives from Italian *sei*, 'six', with the same kind of diminutive ending as for the **sestino** (below).

sestertium
A money of account of Ancient Rome equal to 1000 **sestertii** (see below). The name is usually explained as deriving from Latin *mille sestertium*, 'a thousand sestertii', although this exact expression has not been found in classical writings. (However, the more general plural *milia sestertium*, 'thousands of sestertii', was quite common.)

sestertius (sesterce) (plural, sestertii)
The familiar silver coin of Ancient Rome that had a value of 2½ **asses** or a quarter of a **denarius** (itself thus equal to 10 asses). The name derives from Latin *semis tertius*, 'two and a half' (i.e. a value that has a third half, or two and a 'half of the third').

sestino
A billon silver coin of Naples introduced under Ferdinand III, King of Aragon, in the late 15th century. It had a value of one-sixth of a **tornese**, hence its name (from Italian *sei*, 'six'). Compare **sesino** (above).

seufzer
A colloquial name for the 6-**pfennig** coin, of high copper content, that was struck in huge quantities (about 28 million) in 1701 and 1702 by Frederick Augustus I, Elector of Saxony (otherwise Augustus the Strong, King of Poland), as a copy of the debased **sechsers** of Brandenburg. The name means literally 'sigh', 'groan' in German, referring to the diminished purchasing power of the coin, which caused the populace to 'sigh' when using it.

sextans
A bronze coin of Ancient Rome worth one-sixth of an **as**, as its name suggests (Latin *sextans*, 'sixth part').

193

shahi (shaki)

A former small silver (later copper) coin of Persia, current from the 16th to the 19th century. Its name relates directly to 'shah', since it derives from Persian *shāhī*, 'royal' (itself from *shāh*, 'king').

shekel

The familiar name of the main silver coin of the Jews in biblical times, originally a unit of weight equal to one three-thousandths of a **talent**. Its Hebrew name is *sheqel*, this itself deriving from the verb *shāqal*, 'to weigh'. Today, the shekel is the main currency unit and coin of Israel, superseding the Israeli **pound** in 1980.

shilling

The first English shilling was introduced some time after 1504 as a silver coin by Henry VII, when it was originally known as a **testoon**. It was superseded by the 5-**pence** piece in 1971, with the change to a decimal system in Britain, but continued to circulate, with this value, for some years afterwards (as did the **florin** in its new value of 10 decimal pence). The history of the shilling is thus relatively straightforward, unlike its name, which has still not been conclusively explained. There are three possible sources. The word may be related to Old English *scield*, 'shield', with the ending *-ing* as found in other coin names (penny, originally, and **sterling** and **farthing**). Certainly the first English shilling bore a shield on the reverse with the arms of England and France. However, the name 'shilling' was in use long before 1504 to denote a money of account, from at least as early as the 9th century, and because its value (12 pence or one-twentieth of a **pound**) corresponded to, and derived from, that of Roman coinage, it seems quite possible that the name actually relates directly to its Roman predecessor, the **solidus**, and that it was a 'translation' or rendering of this. German coins of the name were also current before the English shilling, and it is likely that in their case the derivation was a Germanic root such as *scell-* or *skell-* meaning 'to resound', 'to ring'. (Compare **penny** and **pengö**.) It is difficult to place these three possibilities in any kind of order of preference, since a reasonable case can be made for any of them.

194

shu

A former monetary unit of Japan equal to one-sixteenth of a **ryo**. The name simply means 'fraction', 'part'. See also **bu**.

sicca (sicca rupee)

The name was originally that of a freshly minted **rupee** of India, which was accepted at a higher value than a worn one. Later, the word was adopted for a rupee struck under the government of Bengal and current from 1793 to 1836. The origin lies in Arabic *sikkah*, 'die for minting'. (Compare **zecchino**.)

siddiki (sadiki)

The name of a former coin of Mysore worth half a **mohur**, issued in 1786 by the Sultan of Mysore, Tipu Sahib, and named after the first caliph, Abu Bakr Siddik.

siebenkopfstücktaler

A name given in the 18th century to the **laubtaler** of Trier, where it was equal to 7 *Kopfstücke* worth 20 **kreuzers** each, i.e. a total of 140 kreuzer. *Kopfstücke*, literally 'head pieces', is here a conventional name for a 20-kreuzer piece.

siebenkreuzer

The name, literally 'seven-**kreuzer** piece', for the Austrian coin that was originally worth 6 kreuzers but had its value raised to 7 in 1693 since it was effectively being rated as this on the home market. Compare the **siebzehnkreuzer** (below).

siebzehnkreuzer

The '17-**kreuzer** piece', the name given to an Austrian coin that was originally worth 15 kreuzers but which during the war with Turkey (1663–4) effectively equalled 18 kreuzers, so in 1695 was officially established with a value of 17 kreuzers.

siglos

The silver coin of Persia from the 5th to 4th century BC. It had a value of one-twentieth of a gold **daric** and derived its name as a Greek form of the Hebrew **shekel**.

silbergroschen
The 'silver **groschen**', or a 19th-century coin of Prussia worth one-thirtieth of a **thaler** and divided into 12 **pfennigs**. The **neugroschen** was very similar to it. Despite its name, the silbergroschen was a billon coin, not a pure silver one.

siliqua (plural, **siliquae**)
The siliqua was originally the smallest unit of weight of Ancient Rome, equal to one-sixth of a scruple, or one one-thousand-seven-hundred-and-twenty-eighth of a Roman **pound** (**libre**), i.e. 0.19 g., or about 0.07 of an ounce. In about AD 324, under Constantine the Great, a coin of the name was struck, which some thirty years later began to oust the **denarius**. The original minuteness of the weight can be seen clearly expressed in the origin of the name, which in Latin meant 'pod', 'husk'. Etymologically, *siliqua* is thus related to modern English 'shell' and 'silicon'.

simoleon
An American slang name for the **dollar**, perhaps for some reason based on 'simon' but influenced by the name of the **napoleon**.

sisto
A name given to the **grosso** struck under Pope Sixtus V in the second half of the 16th century, with a value of 44 **quattrini**. The name relates directly to that of the Pope (in Italian *Sisto*), who introduced a number of economic and financial reforms.

sixain
The French coin that had a value of 6 **deniers**, so was worth half the **douzain**. As a billon piece, it was issued only under Louis XII (1498–1515) and his successor Francis I (1515–47). The name clearly indicates its denomination.

sixpence
The well-known small silver coin of England, first issued under Edward VI in 1551 and circulating in later mintings until 1980, when it ceased to be legal tender.

From 1971, with the introduction of decimal currency, it had a value of 2½ new **pence**. Its name is self-explanatory, and no new decimal coin was issued to correspond to it (as happened with the **shilling**, for example, and the **florin**). The name was used before 1551 as that of a money of account, from at least the 14th century. Almost more than any other English coin, the sixpence has been commemorated affectionately in several popular songs and nursery rhymes, such as 'Sing a song of sixpence', 'I love sixpence, jolly little sixpence', and 'There was a crooked man, and he walked a crooked mile,/He found a crooked sixpence against a crooked stile'. The last of these suggests that some issues of the coin were easily bent: compare the Scottish colloquial name **crookie**. The best known colloquial name of the sixpence was **tanner**.

skilling

The name of both a money of account and a low-value copper coin in Scandinavia and northern Germany, from the 15th century to the 19th. The denomination clearly corresponds exactly to the English **shilling** and German **schilling**.

slug

The name of an unofficial 50-**dollar** gold coin issued privately in California during the gold rush of the mid-19th century. It was a crude piece, in effect a heavy chunk of metal, mostly octagonal in shape but sometimes round. Its name is the ordinary word 'slug' meaning 'mass of material', although in American usage the word is also associated with the 'slug' that is a fake coin for use in a slot machine.

snaphan

The colloquial name of a silver coin of the Netherlands first issued under Charles of Egmond, Duke of Gelders (1492–1538), with a value of 6 **stuivers**. The obverse bore the figure of a horseman, who was frequently referred to in that period as a *snaphan*, or 'robber', 'highwayman', hence the nickname of the coin, which was really a type of **ducat**. (The actual Dutch word, which corresponds to German *Schnapphahn*, could be translated literally in

English as 'snapcock', i.e. someone who 'snaps' your money before you have time to retaliate. There in fact formerly was an English word 'snaphance' in the identical sense.)

sol (plural, **sols** [French], **soles** [Peruvian])
This name operates, or operated, on two levels. First, it was the historic French coin equal to 12 **deniers** or one-twentieth of a **livre** that became the **sou** at the time of the Revolution (late 18th century). Originally it was a gold coin, then a silver, and finally, in the time of Louis XV (18th century), a copper issue. After the Revolution, its value was fixed at one-twentieth of a **franc** (see **sou** itself for more). Then, in more modern times, the sol was the name of the silver coin of Peru that was first struck in 1863 and that was equal to one-tenth of the Peruvian **libra** or **pound**. From 1930, the sol has been the main monetary unit and (gold) coin of Peru, divided into 100 **centavos**. These two types of sol thus have two different origins for their names. The French sol derives from the Roman **solidus**. The Peruvian sol has a name that is the Spanish for 'sun', referring to the representation of the sun on the earliest coin.

solarus
The name of a silver coin of Mantua issued in 1624 to commemorate the beatification of the Italian Jesuit (canonised as a saint in 1726) Aloysius (Luigi) Gonzaga, who died in 1591. The name refers to the radiate sun that the coin bore.

soldino
A small base silver Venetian coin of the 14th century, with a name that is a diminutive of that of the **soldo**.

soldo (plural, **soldi**)
This is the Italian coin and name that corresponded to the French **sol** (or **sou**), and that thus derives its name from the Roman **solidus**. The first silver soldo was issued in the 12th century. Much later it came to have the value of one-twentieth of a **lira**, or 5 **centesimi**, and was finally superseded by the 5-centesimi coin in the 19th century (just as the English **shilling** was replaced a century later

by the 5-**pence** piece). The 5-centesimi coin continued to be known as a soldo well into the 20th century, and possibly the colloquial name is still not quite extinct in some parts of Italy.

solidus (plural, **solidi**)

This was the standard gold coin of Ancient Rome introduced by Constantine the Great in the early 4th century in place of the **aureus**. It had a value of one seventy-second of a Roman **pound (libra)**, or one-sixth of an **uncia**, and from then on was to become the standard monetary unit of both the Roman Republic and, subsequently, Byzantium. Its name means what it says, 'solid', that is 'thick' as a 'substantial' or 'weighty' piece. As a money of account, the solidus came to be divided into 12 **denarii** (or silver **pennies** of the time), and in this role it was followed by the English **shilling** (as well as the French **sou** and Italian **soldo**): hence the abbreviation 's.' for shilling in '£.s.d.' (or 'L.S.D.'), with the '£' from libra (pound) and the 'd.' from denarius (penny).

somalo

A monetary unit and coin of Somalia from 1950 to 1960, when it was superseded by the Somali **shilling**. The name is obviously derived directly from that of the country and its people.

sophiendukat (sophiendukaten)

The name of a **ducat**-type coin struck by Sophia, mother of John George (Johann Georg) I, Elector of Saxony, at Christmas 1616 for her children. The piece was also known as the *Kinderdukaten*, 'children's ducat', partly referring to the circumstances of the issue, but also deriving directly from the legend on the obverse, which was: WOHL DEM, DER FREUDE AN SEINEN KINDERN ERLEBT ('Blessed is he who has joy from his children'). The coin was struck regularly at the Dresden Mint down to 1872, and was sold as a christening gift for 3½ **thalers**.

sößling (sosling)

The Danish equivalent of the **sechsling** (which see).

199

sou

The more recent name of the French **sol**, popularised at the time of the Revolution in the late 18th century. It was thus the name of the 5-**centime** piece, a sort of equivalent of the English **halfpenny**, and the word became generally used in French for a low-value coin or amount of money, especially to indicate worthlessness (so that today a Frenchman might say *Cela ne vaut pas quatre sous* where an Englishman would say 'It's not worth twopence'). In English itself, too, 'sou' is similarly used, as 'I haven't got a sou left'. Until quite recent times in France, the name was still used colloquially for the 5-centime coin.

souverain (souverain d'or)

A 'gold **sovereign**', or the name of a gold coin of Brabant and the Netherlands struck from the early 17th century until 1832, when it was superseded by Belgian currency. Although the name is French, it is actually a French modification of English 'sovereign' (which itself derived from French, as mentioned below).

sovereign

This is the famous English gold piece first introduced under Henry VII in 1489, when it had a value of 20 **shillings**. It was intended to be a double **rose noble**, or **ryal**, and to serve thus as a coin worth a **pound**, which until then had merely been a money of account. Under Edward VI, in the second half of the 16th century, the sovereign became a 30-shilling piece. Subsequently, under Elizabeth I, a 20-shilling piece was also struck, with this actually being called a pound to distinguish it from the sovereign. However, although other coins worth 20 shillings were minted later, such as the **unite**, there was no actual coin called 'sovereign' from 1660 to 1817, when the first of the modern sovereigns was struck. (During this period, the main English gold coin was the **guinea**.) Sovereigns ceased to be legal tender in the First World War, although they have been struck since then for sale on the international market. The name itself is clearly a 'royal' one, like that of the **crown**, but specifically refers to the depiction of the king (Henry VII) seated on his throne, as appeared on the obverse of the first issue. The actual word 'sovereign', meaning 'supreme ruler', derives from French, with an ultimate origin in Latin *super*, 'over', 'above', although influenced in its spelling by 'reign'. The **souverain d'or** (see above) was closely modelled on the English 30-shilling sovereign.

spadaccino

The colloquial name of the **giulio** struck at Massa Lombarda, Italy, in the 16th century. The name is Italian for 'swordsman' (from Italian *spade*, 'sword'), and refers to the figure of St Paul armed with a sword illustrated on the coin.

spade guinea

The name of a **guinea** issued under George III (1760–1820), referring to the spade-shaped shield on its reverse. The piece was struck from 1787 to 1799.

spadino

The name of a silver **scudo** of Savoy, struck under Charles Emmanuel (Carlo Emanuele) I, Duke of Savoy, in 1630. The word is Italian for 'short sword', and refers to the reverse of the coin which depicted an arm holding a sword.

speciedaler (speciesdaler)

The term for the double **thaler** of Denmark issued in the first half of the 18th century, so called to indicate that it was an actual coin (the sense of 'specie') rather than a banknote, as was more usual for this period.

speigroschen

Literally a 'spit groschen', and the colloquial (and hardly complimentary) name for a 3-**kreuzer** piece of 1736 on which, as the result of a faulty die, a blemish appears under the mouth of Charles of Bavaria (Charles VII), Elector of Bavaria (1726–45), portrayed on it.

spesmilo (plural, spesmiloj)

The name is that of an international currency proposed in 1907 by the Swiss-French philologist and promoter of Esperanto, René de Saussure, and that same year the unit was adopted by the German industrial chemist

201

Herbert F. Höveler for the worldwide Esperanto Cheque Bank founded by him. The proposed divisions of the spesmilo were to be 10 spesdekoj (plural of spesdeko), otherwise 100 spescentoj, otherwise 1000 spesoj. As thus used by Esperantists before the First World War, the spesmilo equalled 50 American **cents**, 1 Russian **rouble**, or 2½ Swiss **francs**. Coins worth 1 and 2 spesmiloj were struck for Saussure in 1912. On one side they bore the head of Ludwig Zamenhof, the Polish inventor of Esperanto in 1887, together with the words L. L. ZAMENHOF, AŬTORO DE ESPERANTO, and on the other they carried the denomination together with a five-pointed star (the Esperanto movement's main symbol), a flaming torch, and the words JUBILEO DE ESPERANTO 1887–1912. Although one A. Holzhaus, in an article in the July 1967 edition of the Esperanto journal *L'Omnibuso*, maintains that the name of the spesmilo may relate to French *espèces* or English 'specie' (both meaning 'coined money'), it seems more likely that the first half of the word derives directly from that of 'Esperanto' itself. This was actually the pseudonym of Zamenhof, and meant 'hoping one' (compare Latin *spes*, 'hope', French *espérer*, 'to hope', and related words in other languages). The second half of the name means 'thousand' (as Latin *mille*, French *mille* and so on). It seems rather strange that the basic name of the new unit was not simply 'spes', with 'spesmilo' serving for a value one-thousandth of this. Dealings in the currency were made difficult by the outbreak of the war, and in 1918 the Bank was wound up. The concept of an international currency was revived, however, in the **stelo** (which see). Compare also the **écu** for a similar unit outside the artificial Esperanto one.

spitzgroschen

The colloquial name of a **groschen** struck under Prince Ernest, Elector of Saxony (1464–86), together with his brothers Albert and William. The name refers to the obverse of the coin, which showed the Landsberg crest in a triangle decorated with three pointed leaves (German *Spitz*, 'point'). Although originally a nickname, the designation later became official.

sprat
A slang name in the 19th century for the English **sixpence**, indicating a small coin or 'tiddler'.

sprenger
A colloquial name in Germany in the second half of the 16th century for a silver coin of Liège (German: Lüttich) that was worth 5 **patards**, or a quarter of a **thaler**. The name is German for 'spray', and refers to the floral cross on the reverse.

srebenik (serebryanik)
The earliest known Russian silver coin, struck at the end of the 10th century from the silver (Russian *serebro*) obtained by melting down Arabic coins. The name really relates not so much to the silver itself, but to the inscription encircling the portrait of Prince Vladimir of Novgorod, which ran: VLADIMIR NA STOLE – A SE EGO SREBRO ('Vladimir is on his throne – and this is his silver'). The srebenik bore no denominational value.

staatendaalder
A silver **daalder** introduced in the Spanish Netherlands in 1578 by Philip II of Spain, with a value of two 16-**stuiver** pieces (introduced the previous year), or 1 **gulden** (**guilder**), 12 stuivers. The name simply means 'state daalder', 'official daalder'. Compare **staatenschilling** (below).

staatenschilling
A **schilling** struck in 1672 in the United (Dutch) Netherlands, except in the provinces of West Frisia, Zeeland and Holland. The name merely declares the piece to be an 'official' or 'state' issue (compare **staatendaalder**, above).

stäbler
The colloquial name of a **pfennig** struck at Basle in 1373 as a **bracteate** piece. The name refers to the staff or rod (German *Stab*) that appeared in the Basle coat of arms on the coin.

stag

A slang name for the English **shilling** in the 19th century. The term seems to relate to the common use of the denomination for commercial deals or calculations; compare the modern 'stag' who is a speculator on the Stock Exchange.

stampee

A colloquial name for the base metal **sou** circulating in the French West Indies during the second half of the 18th century. The coin was countermarked or 'stamped' for use by British traders there.

stanislas d'or (stanislausdor)

The name of a gold **pistole** struck in 1794 under Stanislas II Augustus, King of Poland.

stater

A disagreeably vague word for any standard gold or silver coin of Ancient Greece, of whatever size or value. The name itself is simply Greek for 'standard coin', from the verb *histanai*, 'to stand'. In actual fact, many coins called a stater turn out to have been a double denomination of some kind.

steckenreiter

The colloquial name of a **ducat** of Nürnberg, struck in 1650 to commemorate the Peace of Westphalia (1648). The reverse of the piece showed a boy riding a hobby horse, hence the name (from German *Steckenpferd*, 'hobby horse').

steinbockpfennig

The name of a coin of the **pfennig** type first struck under Albert IV, Duke of Austria (1395–1404) in order to boost the flagging economy, with the new coin replacing any existing pfennig that had been in circulation for over fifty years. German *Steinbock* means 'mountain goat', 'ibex', and this animal was depicted on the piece.

stella

A so called 'goloid' (gold, copper and silver combined) coin of the United States with a value of 4 **dollars**

204

planned in the second half of the 19th century as an international issue designed to tie the US coinage to the Latin Monetary Union (between Belgium, France, Italy and Switzerland) formed in 1865. The aim was to have a standardised coinage system, with the stella thus equal to 20 French **francs**, 8 Austrian **florins**, 8 Dutch **guilders**, 20 Italian **lire**, and 20 Spanish **pesetas**. Only a few were produced, however (the largest minting in 1879), so that today the piece is a collector's item. The name, Latin for 'star', refers to the central feature on the reverse of the coin, a five-pointed star, representing the envisaged union of the five countries. Compare **stelo** (below).

stellino
A type of **testoon** struck in 1554 under Cosimo I, Duke of Florence. The name derives from Italian *stella*, 'star', and refers to the small star next to the bust portrait of the Duke that appeared on the obverse.

stelo
An international currency unit proposed after the Second World War by the Esperanto movement, broadly on the same basis as that of the earlier **spesmilo** which failed to be realised as a result of the First World War. Coins were issued for both single and multiple values, and each bore a five-pointed star (Esperanto *stelo*), the symbol of the movement. For a similar concept, see also **écu**.

sterling

Today the name is almost exclusively associated (apart from its general sense of 'genuine', 'worthy') with the currency of Britain, especially the **pound** sterling as the British pound worth 100 **pence**. Originally, however, the name was used of a number of small silver coins in medieval times, in particular the silver penny, and it seems to have been intended to denote the purity and fine quality of such coins. The actual etymology of the word is still disputed. It is sometimes said to derive from 'easterling' (or some similar spelling) as the name or title of a Hanseatic merchant, who would thus have come to England from the east and brought coins with him. But the term 'sterling' (more exactly as Medieval Latin *sterlingus*) was first recorded before the time of such merchants, and so rules this explanation out. It is possible that the derivation lies in French *esterlin* or *esterling*, as the name used by the Normans for the penny circulating in the time of William the Conqueror (11th century) and subsequently. But this may well have been a borrowing from the English. Other etymologists and numismatists have favoured a source in 'starling', with reference to the four birds seen on many coins current in the reign of Edward the Confessor (11th century), or in Old English *strong* or *strang*, 'strong', alluding to the 'strength' or reliability of the coin as a basic currency. However, most experts now tend to favour another explanation, which is that the name represents 'star' (Old English *steorra*, Old French *estoile*, Latin *stella*). If this is so, the reference would thus be to the distinctive star that some medieval pennies certainly bore. The ending *-ing* may have developed by association with other coin names such as **farthing** and **shilling**. Early spellings of 'penny', too, have been recorded as some variant of *pening*. The general meaning of the word today in its sense of 'excellent' ('sterling work' and the like) comes from the name of the coin, but was not commonly in use until as late as the 17th century.

stiefelknecht

The jocular name of a **groschen** (also a half-groschen) struck in 1764 by Frederick the Great, which bore the initial letters of his name 'FR' inscribed in a classical style (technically known as 'antique'). The bold, open form of the letter 'R' looked something like a bootjack (German *Stiefelknecht*), hence the name.

stiver

An English spelling of **stuiver**, actually used on some coins issued in Ceylon (now Sri Lanka) in the early 19th century.

stooter (stoter)

A base silver coin of the Netherlands, first struck in the second half of the 16th century with a value of one-twentieth of a **daalder**, or 2½ **stuivers**. The Dutch name literally means 'pusher', 'stamper', from *stoten*, 'to push', 'to stamp', simply indicating a coin that has been officially minted. It was current in the United (Dutch) Provinces for about seventy years.

stotinka (plural, stotinki)
A main monetary unit of Bulgaria, one hundred of which make up a **lev**. It was introduced when the country joined the Latin Monetary Union (see **stella**) in 1880, and there is still a 1-stotinka coin. The name derives directly from Bulgarian *sto*, 'hundred'.

straubenpfennig
The name of a base **pfennig** struck in the 16th and 17th centuries in Upper and Lower Saxony. The origin of the name is uncertain: it may derive from the German root *strup* seen in *struppig*, 'rough', 'unkempt' or dialect *struppiert*, 'worn out', or else refer to a mintmaster named Straube who was active at the mint at Frankenhausen in the first half of the 16th century. Some of the pieces issued in about 1620 have the inscription I/STRAV/PHEN, which does not seem to solve the uncertainty.

stüber
A German billon coin struck in the second half of the 15th century in Rhine-Westphalia as a copy of the Netherlands **stuiver**, whose name it acquired in a German variant.

stuiver
The well-known base silver (later, copper) coin of the Netherlands, first struck in the late 15th century and worth one-twentieth of a **gulden (guilder)**. There are two possible theories behind the name. One derives it from some Germanic word related to modern German *stumpf*, 'blunt' and modern English 'stub', referring to the relative thickness or 'dumpiness' of the piece. The other takes it from Dutch *stuiven*, 'to scatter', 'to spark out', with reference to the rays that emanate from the chain of the Order of the Golden Fleece, which was represented on it. The second seems the more likely, and is supported by the fact that the French name of the 3-stuiver piece known in Dutch as the **vlies**, which bore the same regalia, was **briquet** (which see), as it was for the **vuurijzer**.

styca
A name given in fairly modern times to a base metal coin of the 7th to 9th centuries, found in Northumbria as a debased form of the **sceat**. Despite the similarity between the names, they are of different origins, and the styca, although also an Old English word, meant simply 'piece (of money)', related to modern German *Stück*, 'piece' (with *Geldstück* meaning 'coin').

sucre
The major monetary unit of Ecuador, a silver **crown**-sized piece introduced in 1884 with a value of 100 **centavos**. The name is that of the South American liberator and general, Antonio José de Sucre (1795–1830), whose portrait was on the coin. The name is pronounced 'sookray'.

sueldo
A former monetary unit and coin of Bolivia, first struck in 1827 as a silver piece with a value of 1 **real**, or one-eighth of a **peso**. The name is the Spanish equivalent of the Italian **soldo**, thus deriving ultimately from the Roman **solidus**.

sultanin (sultany)
A former Turkish gold coin, struck in the 16th and 17th centuries and later, outside Turkey, in Algiers and Tunis. The name is an Arabic one meaning 'sultany', 'kingdom', so is in the 'royal' category.

sword and sceptre piece
The name of a Scottish gold coin struck in the early 17th century with a value of 8 Scottish **pounds**, or 10 English **shillings**. The name describes the reverse, which showed a crossed sword and sceptre under a crown.

sword dollar
A colloquial name for the silver **rial** (or **ryal**) of Scotland, as struck under James VI in the second half of the 16th century. The name comes from the reverse of the coin, which showed a crowned sword pointing upwards to the value ('XXX', i.e. 30 Scottish **shillings**).

From 1582 the reverse had a bust of the king with a drawn sword.

syli

The main monetary unit and coin of Guinea, divided into 100 cauries (this name representing the former cowrie shells that served as currency). It was introduced in 1972 to replace the Guinea **franc**, and the name is a native (Susu) one, meaning 'elephant', the symbol of the Guinea Democratic Party. There are currently coins with a denomination of half a syli, 1 syli, 2 and 5 sylis, with notes for higher values, but no currency representing the caurie at all.

szostak

A former silver (later, copper) coin of Poland, first struck in 1528 with a value of 6 **groszy**. There were various issues down to the 19th century. The name simply indicates the denomination, deriving from Polish *sześć*, 'six'.

T

tael (tale)

This is the common European name used for the standard silver weight in the Chinese monetary system, formerly divided into 10 **mace** or 100 **candareens**. The name derives, through Portuguese, from Malay *tahil*, 'weight', itself probably from Hindi *tolā*, the term used for the weight of a **sicca rupee**, and in turn from a Sanskrit root that ultimately lies behind modern English 'tolerate'.

taka

The main monetary unit and coin of Bangladesh, introduced in 1972 instead of the Pakistani **rupee**. It equals 100 **paise** and has a name that ultimately derives, through Bengali, from Sanskrit *ṭaṅka*, 'coin' (compare **tanga**, **tangka** and **tankah**, below).

tala (plural, same)

The main monetary unit of Western Samoa, introduced in 1967 to replace the Samoan **pound**. The name is a Samoan modification of **dollar** in the same way that the name of the **sene**, its one-hundredth part, is a variant of **cent**.

talari

A former silver coin of Ethiopia, last struck in 1904. It was introduced under Menelik II, Emperor of Ethiopia, in 1892, when it was based on the **Maria Theresa thaler**, and so derives its name from this earlier coin.

talent

The talent was originally an ancient unit of weight, adopted by various races and countries from its source in

Babylonia. Subsequently it became a monetary unit with a value equal to its weight in gold or silver. Among the best known talents are the one of Palestine and Syria, equal to 3000 **shekels**, and the unit of Ancient Greece equal to 6000 **drachmai**. Whatever the precise value in weight or money, the origin of the name derives from Greek *talenton*, 'weight', itself ultimately related to modern English 'tolerate'. (In this connection, compare **tael**, above.) The general sense of 'talent' today, to mean 'gift', 'aptitude', derives from the Parable of the Talents in the Bible (Matthew 25:14–30) where the 'talents' are actual coins.

tallero

The name began as an Italian word for the German **thaler**, then later became that of an independent coin of Italy struck in the late 16th century at Venice and Modena for trade with the Middle East. The tallero struck at Venice in 1756 was a close copy of the **Maria Theresa thaler**, while the earlier tallero of Modena, struck in 1650, was modelled on the Netherlands **leeuwendaalder** (which the Italians called the *tallero leoncino*). The tallero or *tallero eritreo* was also the name of a silver coin struck in Rome and Milan in 1890 for the Italian colony of Eritrea (now a province of Ethiopia). This was also a thaler-type piece and had a value of 5 **lire**. It ceased to be issued in 1941.

tambala (plural, same)

A main monetary unit and coin of Malawi, equal to one-hundredth of a **kwacha**. Both units were introduced in 1971, with the adoption of a decimal system. The name of the tambala is a native one, meaning 'cockerel'. The bird crows at dawn, and is thus symbolic of a new life and 'coming of light'. Compare the **kwacha**.

tanga

A former copper (originally silver) coin of the Portuguese East Indies, struck from the early 17th century with a value of one-fifth of a **xeraphim**. The name is a Hindi one, deriving from Sanskrit *ṭaṅka*, 'weight', 'coin'. Compare **taka** (above) and **tangka** and **tankah** (below).

tangka

A basic silver monetary unit of Tibet, said to have been first struck in Nepal in the 16th century. Like the **tanga** (above) and **tankah** (below) the name is ultimately a Sanskrit one, meaning 'weight', 'coin'.

tankah

The name used of a number of gold and silver coins of India, especially those current from the 12th century to the 16th, when the Moguls introduced the **mohur** and the **rupee**. As with the two names above, the origin, through Hindi, is in Sanskrit *ṭaṅka*, 'weight', 'coin'.

tanner

A colloquial or slang name for the English **sixpence**, current from the early 19th century (possibly earlier) to the demise of the coin itself in the second half of the 20th century. There has been much speculation regarding the origin of the name, some more ingenuous than ingenious, but on balance it does perhaps seem more likely to have derived from a personal name Tanner (one John Tanner, an engraver at the Mint, is usually cited) than as a corruption of **danaro** or Romany (Gypsy) *tano*, 'little'. Much wit and ink has been similarly devoted to the biblical 'one Simon a tanner' (Acts 10:32), especially as 'simon' has also been recorded as a slang word for a sixpence. But it must surely be unwise to direct too much scholarly attention to such a coincidental, if enjoyable coupling. (Readers who are tempted nonetheless should read Eric Partridge's dissertation on the subject, in his *Adventuring Among Words*, pp 51–2.)

tari

The name of a gold coin of Italy, struck in southern Italy from the 10th century. The origin of the name has not been conclusively established, but it is possibly a modification of the name of the Arabic **dirham**.

terzarola

A gold coin of Genoa, issued in the first half of the 14th century under Simon Boccanegra, Doge of Genoa. It had a value of a third of a **genovino**, and derives its name from Italian *terza*, 'third', 'third part'.

213

tester

The colloquial name of a **sixpence** in Shakespeare's day (early 17th century), originating as a corrupted or deliberately perverted name of the **testoon** (or **teston**) of the time of Henry VII, i.e. the early 16th-century **shilling**. It is still not exactly clear why the latter name became the former, although there seems to have been some connection with the general depreciation of currency at that time.

teston

The French version of the **testoon**, otherwise a silver coin introduced by Louis XII in 1513 after he had struck the **testone** for his Italian possessions. The piece replaced the **gros tournois**. For the origin of the name, see **testoon** (below).

testone

The Italian version of the **testoon** (which see for the origin of the name). The first coin of the designation was the one struck under Galeazzo Maria Sforza, Duke of Milan, in 1474. This was a copy of the Venetian **lira** trono (see **trono**), issued two years earlier, and it was the first to bear the name generally. This Italian spelling is often used for the **teston** struck by Louis XII for his Italian possessions of Asti, Milan and Genoa (see previous entry).

testoon

The English version of the **teston** and **testone** (above), both of which preceded it. The name is usually given to the **shilling** introduced by Henry VII in 1594 (see **tester**, above), and to the silver coin of Scotland equal to 4 Scottish shillings that was struck from 1553 to 1562. This was a copy of the Italian testone. The English testoon of 1504 was the first to bear the portrait of the reigning monarch, which gives added point to the name, since it derives, through Old French, from the Italian (*testone*), which is simply an augmentative of *testa*, 'head', referring to the monarch's head that the coin bore (in the case of the original piece, the rather handsome one of the Duke of Milan).

214

tetradrachm

As the name indicates, a 4-**drachma** coin of Ancient Greece, and the largest standard silver piece in the series. The coin bore no denominational value.

tetrobol

Like the **tetradrachm** (above), the name is self-explanatory, here indicating a 4-**obol** piece of Ancient Greece, equal to two-thirds of a **drachma**.

thaler

The famous predecessor and progenitor of the 'almighty **dollar**'. Its origin lies in Tyrol and Bohemia, where in the 15th century a need arose for larger silver coins to exploit the growth in trade and commerce. A number of large silver mines were opened up for this purpose, and resulted in the minting of German pieces then called **guldengroschen**, implying that although actually silver coins, they had a silver content equal to that of a gold **gulden**. In 1518 the first such pieces were minted in silver from the newly opened and richly endowed mine at Joachimsthal ('St Joachim's valley'), now Jáchymov in north-west Czechoslovakia. These coins bore a figure of St Joachim (according to non-biblical tradition, the father of the Virgin Mary), and within a few years the generic name *Thaler* (or *Taler*) had developed from the latter part of the mine's name. The coin and its name became popular on a virtually international scale (see Appendix II, p. 243, for some varieties of it), and for some four hundred years the thaler was *the* standard European silver coin. The first American dollar, as a development of the name, was struck in 1794, and was issued as a silver coin until 1935. This particular name is sometimes said to have been a deliberate modification of thaler by President-to-be Jefferson, who similarly proposed **cent**, **dime** (as *disme*), **eagle** and **mill**, with varying degrees of originality in 1785. But the spelling 'dollar' was a natural anglicisation of the German word, and had been current in English for almost two hundred years before Jefferson made his choice of coin names. (What Jefferson actually wrote in his *Notes on a Money Unit for the United States*, published in 1782, was: 'The unit or dollar is a known coin and the most familiar of all to the

215

mind of the people. It is already adopted from south to north.' He was here referring to the Spanish **peso**, or **piece of eight**, which was that country's equivalent to the thaler, just as England's was the **crown**, France's the **écu**, and Russia's the **rouble**.) In all these names, the name of the man who first issued the prototype thalers at Joachimsthal is sometimes overlooked. He was Baron Schlick, member of a wealthy titled Bohemian family, whose name was, however, commemorated in the alternative designation of *Schlicktaler* for the piece.

thebe

One of the two main monetary units and coins of Botswana, introduced in 1976 as one-hundredth of a **pula**. The name is a native (Setswana) one, meaning 'shield'. The coin is thus one of the most recent members of the French **écu** family (see Appendix II, p. 243), and actually bears the shield of Botswana on the reverse.

threepence

Like the **sixpence**, a straightforward and obvious name, in this case for the former silver coin first struck in England under Edward VI in 1551. In 1937 the little silver coin, a favourite 'find' in a Christmas pudding, was replaced by the larger, heavier nickel-brass twelve-sided piece with the characteristic 'thrift' design (the plant, designed to represent the attribute), with the name often occurring in the form 'threepenny piece' or 'threepenny bit'. The last issue of this type (the one with the portcullis design) was in 1967, and the coin ceased to be legal tender when the old **penny** did, in 1971, with the introduction of decimalisation.

thrymsa (thrimsa)

An English gold coin of the Anglo-Saxon period, struck in the 6th or 7th century. It was based on the Roman **triens**, in particular the later version of this known as the **tremissis**, and the English name was almost certainly derived from this last, which was itself known in Late Latin as the *tremis*. (There has been some grammatical distortion of the original, however, since as it stands 'thrymsa' represents the Old English genitive plural, used after a numeral, of a form *trimes* or *trims*, and this was

216

apparently taken by 17th-century antiquarians to be a nominative singular. Hence the alteration in the ending.)

tical (tecal, tycal, tickal, tekal)

In modern times, the tical has been one of the main monetary units and coins of Thailand (see **baht**, its present equivalent name). Originally, it was the so-called 'bullet money' of Siam (as Thailand was then known), Cambodia (modern Kampuchea) and Burma, a strangely shaped small coin like a little ingot or 'bullet', hammered into a spherical shape and crudely flattened at the side. The name itself goes back via Thai to Malay *tikal*, 'monetary unit', in turn from Sanskrit *tarkala*, 'stamped (silver) coin'. Some etymologists equate the word with the Sanskrit *ṭaṅka*, 'weight', 'coin', that gave the names of the **tanga**, **tangka** and **tankah** (see above), amongst others.

ticky (tickey)

A former name for a **threepence** piece in South Africa, current in the 19th century. The term is probably a native modification of some European word, such as English 'ticket', Dutch *stukje*, 'little piece', 'small coin', or Portuguese **pataca** (itself a corruption of a non-European word). The 'ticket' origin is explained by the *Oxford English Dictionary* as follows: 'On an occasion when a large body of natives were employed on a public work, they were, for want of small silver coin, paid with tickets for 3d., which were taken in payment by the provision stores, and redeemed at that rate by the authorities'. However, no final origin has been conclusively established, and it is not impossible that the word may have been simply an attempt to say 'little' or something similar (although not 'itsy-bitsy' or 'titchy' which are too recent, and anyway too characteristically 'English').

tientje

The name of a gold coin of the Netherlands, struck in the 19th century at a value of 10 **gulden** (**guilders**). The issue continued into the 20th century, with mintings in gold between 1925 and 1933, but with a silver piece struck in 1970 to mark the twenty-fifth anniversary of the end of the Second World War. The name is really 'tenner', from

Dutch *tien*, 'ten'. The Germans called it *das holländische Zehnguldenstück*, 'the Dutch ten-guilder piece'.

tizzy

A former slang word for an English **sixpence**, current in the 19th century. The origin of the name is uncertain, and although similar to that of the **ticky**, is unlikely to be connected with it. Perhaps it somehow evolved from **tester** or **testoon**.

tlaco

A small copper coin of Mexico in the 19th century, equal to half a **cuartilla**, i.e. a quarter of a **real**. The name is a native Indian one (Nahuatl), meaning 'half'. Since there was an acute shortage of small change, some tlacos were 'struck' not out of copper at all, but from cardboard, glass, leather, and non-precious metals.

toman

Originally a money of account, the toman was struck as the principal gold coin of Persia from the late 18th century, down to which time the main gold piece had been the **mohur**. It had a value of 10,000 **dinars**, and the name relates to this, as probably deriving, through Persian, from a Tatar word for 'ten thousand'.

tornese (plural, **tornesi**)

The Italian name of the French **gros tournois**, and for an independent Italian coin based on it, struck in the late 15th century. Multiple tornesi were minted down to the latter half of the 17th century. The name simply derives from the Italian for 'of Tours' (the French town that gave its name to the gros tournois). Compare the **tornez** (below).

tornez

A silver coin of Portugal, struck under Peter (Pedro) I in the second half of the 14th century and modelled on the French **gros tournois**. The name is the Portuguese equivalent of Italian **tornese** (see above).

tostão

A silver coin of Portugal first struck under Emanuel (Manuel) I (1495–1521) as an imitation of the Italian **testone**, whose name it modified accordingly. Unlike the original testone, however, the tostão did not show the king's head on the obverse, but instead had the Portuguese arms (on a shield under a crown). Bearing in mind the fact that Italian *testone* means 'head', this therefore makes the tostão something of a misnomer!

tremissis (plural, **tremisses**) (**tremis**)

A late variation of the Roman **triens**, and itself a gold coin of Byzantium, worth a third of a **solidus**. From this in turn derived the Frankish tremissis current from about the 6th century to the 8th. The name is a Late Latin one formed as a contraction of *tres*, 'three' and **semis** (which see). This implies 'third of an **as**', as does the name of the triens itself (see below).

triens

The name of an early bronze coin of Ancient Rome, equal to a third of an **as**, as its name indicates (from Latin *tres*, 'three'). It was issued from the end of the 4th century BC, and later became a gold coin with a value of a third of a **solidus** (see **tremissis**, above).

trime

The silver 3-**cent** coin of the United States issued from 1851 to 1873, with a name based on that of the **dime** (value 10 cents).

triobol

A silver coin of Ancient Greece with a value, as its name indicates, of three **obols**, i.e. half a **drachma**.

trionfo

A gold coin of the Venetian **zecchino** (**sequin**) type, first apparently struck in the reign of Ferdinand I, King of Aragon (1412–16), in Sicily. The name is Italian for 'triumph', and presumably was intended as a 'grand' designation for a royal issue.

trojak
A silver coin of Poland with a value of three **groszy** (**groschen**), first struck in 1528. From the 18th century it was a copper coin and circulated widely in the Ukraine and Belorussia. Its name means simply 'three-er'.

tronetto
A money of account of Trento, Italy (now South Tirol or Alto Adige), corresponding to 1 **lira** and equal to 12 **kreuzers** (14½ after 1813). The name relates to its region of origin. It should not be confused with that of the **trono** (below) even though that was also a lira.

trono (lira trono)
Originally a money of account corresponding to a **lira** (from the 10th century); the coin was first struck, and acquired its name, in the second half of the 15th century, when it was issued in Venice under the Doge of Venice, Niccolò Trono. The obverse bore a bust of the Doge, and the reverse a Venetian lion in a laurel wreath. These depictions were later regarded as unworthy of the Venetian republic and were replaced, respectively, by a figure of St Mark with the Doge kneeling, on the obverse, and a standing figure of Christ on the reverse.

tsien
The Chinese name of the coin and currency usually known in English as **cash**. The name means literally 'horn', 'angle', 'corner' and is generally also the standard Chinese word for 'money'. Compare **sen**, its Japanese equivalent.

tugrik
The main monetary unit and coin of Mongolia, divided into 100 **mungu**. The first coins of the name were struck in Leningrad in 1925 as silver pieces. The name represents Mongolian *dughurik*, literally 'round thing', 'wheel', hence 'coin'.

turner
An alternative name for the Scottish **bodle** (a variety of 2-**penny** coin of the 18th century), probably deriving as an alteration of French *tournois* (as for the **gros**

tournois), with reference to the double tournois (see **double**) circulating in France in the 17th century, which it resembled. In the past, the name has sometimes been corrupted as 'turnover'.

tympf

The name of the **achtzehngroschen** struck in base silver in the 17th century and circulating in Poland and Prussia, also known as the **guldentympf** (which was a **gulden** originally worth 30 **groschen** but with an actual value, stamped on it, of 18). The name, which became synonymous with a debased coin, is that of the Polish mintmaster of German extraction, Andreas Tympf, who issued the piece from about 1652 to 1667. The tympf continued to be struck in Prussia down to the Seven Years' War (1756–63), during which it became so devalued that many people refused to use it, and in 1765 it ceased to be minted.

U

uncia (plural, **unciae**)

In Ancient Rome, the uncia was originally a weight equal to one-twelfth of a **pound** (**libra**), with a subsequent copper coin being the same fraction of an **as**. English 'ounce' is a development from the Latin name, which itself is based on *unus*, 'one', 'unit' (i.e. one part of the whole pound). There has been no English coin named 'ounce', although the word has been used to translate the Spanish **onza**.

ungaro

An Italian name for the Hungarian **ducat**, or for a subsequent Italian coin modelled on it, as widely struck in northern Italy in the 17th century. The name is simply Italian for 'Hungarian'.

unicorn

A gold coin of Scotland, struck under James III in 1486 and later under James IV and V (to 1517). The piece has a value of 18 Scottish **shillings**, and derived its name from the unicorn with crown and shield depicted on the obverse. The former royal arms of Scotland were supported by two unicorns, and from 1603, when James VI of Scotland became also King of England (as James I), he 'imported' one of them to support the British shield together with the English lion (where it supplanted the red dragon of Wales).

unierijksdaalder

A 'union **rijksdaalder**', or the name of a **daalder** of the Netherlands struck in the second half of the 16th century by the Earl of Leicester, who was Stadholder (chief magistrate) of the Netherlands for eleven years from

1586. The 'union' is that of the United Provinces, formed by the Union of Utrecht in 1579 and declaring their independence (from the Spanish Netherlands) in 1581, i.e. when the Protestant northern provinces split from the Catholic southern ones.

unite

A gold coin of England and Scotland, struck in 1604 by James I of England (James VI of Scotland) to celebrate the union of the two kingdoms. The name obviously relates to this but derived more directly from the Latin legend on the piece, which was: FACIAM EOS IN GENTEM VNAM ('I will make them one people', a biblical quotation from Ezekiel 37:22). The coin had a value of 20 **shillings** and resembled the earlier **sovereign**. (The name is pronounced with the first syllable stressed, as in 'unity'.)

utuzlik

A silver coin of the Turkish (Ottoman) Empire, with a value of 30 **paras**. The name is that of its denomination, from Turkish *utuz*, 'thirty' (compare **altmishlik**).

V

vatu

The sole monetary unit and coin of Vanuatu (formerly New Hebrides), introduced in 1981 to replace the Vanuatu (formerly New Hebridean) **franc**. The name derives from that of the country (whose own name means 'our land').

venustaler

The name of a **thaler** struck in 1622 to commemorate the foundation of Magdeburg as an archiepiscopal see in 962 (although the name is recorded at least a century earlier). The city has a name that itself has long been popularly interpreted as 'maiden's town' (German *Magd*, 'maid'), with one of the oldest churches, the Liebfrauenkirche ('Church of the Virgin'). Venus was the Roman goddess of love and beauty, a personification of maidenhood, and was presumably chosen for the coin, where she is represented with the three Graces, as a suitable figurehead for the town with its existing 'maidenly' associations. The precise depiction on the reverse of the thaler is that of two doves and two swans pulling a chariot in which Venus and the Graces are standing. This produced the hardly ladylike popular name for the coin, which was *Hurenkarrentaler*, 'whore-cart thaler'.

vertugadin

The colloquial name for the silver **écu** of France, worth 5 **livres**, that was issued under Louis XV in 1715 and subsequently. Louis was only five years old at the time, and the coin represents him by way of portraying a young draped head. This fancifully resembled a farthingale, or the petticoat over one, hence the name (with French *vertugadin*, 'farthingale' actually giving the English word, which was corrupted in the process).

victoria

A proposed English coin planned to equal 10 **mills** in a possible decimal issue at the end of the 19th century. In its issue for June 1896, the *Westminster Review* wrote: 'Let the $\frac{1}{1000}$ of a pound, the coin to be issued in lieu of the farthing, be called a "mill", and let ten of these make a "victoria".' The plan was never realised. The name, like many names of the period, was obviously a tribute to Queen Victoria, the reigning monarch. It could also, however, have been intended as an echo of Roman coinage, where some pieces bore a figure of the goddess of victory (Victoria). See **victoriatus** (below).

victoriatus (victoriate)

A silver coin of Ancient Rome, smaller than the **denarius**, first struck in the second Punic War (3rd century BC) and having a reverse that bore the figure of Victoria, the goddess of victory, crowning a trophy. Its value was three-quarters of a denarius (later half a denarius). See also **victoria** (above).

viente

A colloquial name for a silver coin of Cuba worth 20 **centavos**, introduced in 1915. The name is simply Spanish for 'twenty'. Compare **vintem** (below).

vierer

A 'fourer', or a 4-**pfennig** silver coin current from 1397 to the end of the 15th century in Strasbourg. The issue was continued at various Swiss mints later than this.

vierlander

The name of a double **groschen** or **patard**, struck under Philip the Good, Duke of Burgundy, some time after 1433 in the four provinces of Brabant, Flanders, Holland and Hainaut. Hence the name, which means 'four provinces'.

vierling

A 'quarter', or a coin worth a quarter of a **pfennig** struck no earlier than the 12th century with the aim of fulfilling a need for small change values. The name is on a par with that of the **farthing**.

vintem

A silver coin of Portugal, first struck in 1489 under John II with the value of one **real**. The name does not relate to this but to a subsequent copper issue of the 17th century, worth 20 copper **reis**. Portuguese *vintem* simply means 'twenty'. (Compare **viente**, above, and **vintina**, below.)

vintina (ventina)

A silver coin with a value of 20 **soldi**, issued in Corsica in the 18th century. The name relates directly to the denomination (French *vingt*, Italian *venti*, 'twenty').

vlies

The name of any gold or silver coin of the Netherlands that bore a representation of the Order of the Golden Fleece (Dutch *vlies*), founded by Philip the Good, Duke of Burgundy (see **vierlander**, above) in 1429 to honour his marriage with Isabella of Portugal. See also **stuiver**.

volpetta see **armelino**.

vreneli

A colloquial name for modern (20th-century) gold coins of Switzerland, with value of 10, 20 and 100 **francs**, that have an obverse showing a girl's head under the Latin name of Switzerland, HELVETIA. 'Vreneli' is really a nickname for the girl, and is a diminutive or pet form of 'Veronica'. The different values were struck in various years between 1897 and 1949. The personification of the girl is somewhat similar to that of 'Marianne', the young woman portrayed on French coins and stamps.

vuurijzer

A silver coin of the Netherlands first struck in the second half of the 15th century under Charles the Bold at Nijmegen. The name is Dutch for 'fire-steel' (*vuur*, 'fire', *ijzer*, 'iron', 'steel'), and refers to the sparkling (or even sparking) chain of the Order of the Golden Fleece, which appears on the coin. The French name for it was **briquet** (which see). See also **vlies**.

W

waterlootaler

A commemorative **thaler** issued under George V, the last King of Hanover (1851–66), to mark the fiftieth anniversary of the victory of the British and Prussian forces over Napoleon's 'Belle Alliance' in the Battle of Waterloo (18 June 1815). The obverse bore the head of the King, the reverse had the inscription: DEN SIEGERN BEI WATERLOO GEWIDMET AM 18.JUNI 1865 ('Dedicated to the victors at Waterloo, 18 June 1865').

weidenbaumtaler

Literally a 'weeping willow **thaler**', or the name of a thaler struck in the first half of the 17th century under William V, Landgrave of Hesse-Cassel (1627–37). The reverse of the coin showed a palm-tree in a gust of wind and had the inscription: DEO VOLENTE HUMILIS LEVABOR ('By God's will shall I be humbly raised'). The tree was thought to be a weeping willow, hence the name.

wewelinghöfer

The name of a small double-sided **pfennig** of Westphalia, believed to have been first struck under Frederick II, King of Germany, in the first half of the 13th century. The piece was subsequently issued under various bishops in different cities (the first striking was at Dortmund), and the coin received its name in the second half of the 14th century after one of these, Florenz (Florentius) von Wewelinghofen, Bishop of Münster (1364–79).

wilhelms d'or (wilhelmsdor)

This 'gold William' has been the name of at least three coins: (1) a double Prussian **pistole**, introduced by

Frederick William I, King of Prussia, in 1737; (2) a later pistole struck under William (Wilhelm), Duke of Brunswick (Braunschweig) (1830–84); (3) a gold coin of the Netherlands, known there as a *gouden willem*. The first of the three was the model for the **friedrich d'or**.

witten (witte)

A type of **albus** with a value of 4 **pfennigs**, struck (or at any rate first recorded) in the 14th century as a result of the requirement for coins of higher denomination than just a pfennig. It first appeared in Lübeck, then in various other Hanseatic cities. Its name means what 'albus' does, i.e. 'white' (modern German *weiss*).

won (plural, same)

The main currency unit of North and South Korea, divided respectively into 100 chon (North Korea) and 100 jeon (South). (Both these names are really the same, and mean simply 'coin', 'piece'.) In South Korea, from 1953 to 1962, the official spelling of the name was 'hwan', but this, too, is basically the same as 'won' and so derived from Korean *wån*, 'round' (compare **yang** and **yuan**).

X

xeraphim (seraphin)
A silver coin struck for the Portuguese Indian colonies at Goa and Diu from the late 16th century to the late 19th, with a value of 360 (later 300) **reis** or half a **rupee**. In the final years of issue the piece was known as a **paradao**, and this word actually appeared on it. Even so it continued to be known by its old name, which is a Portuguese corruption of Arabic *sharīfī*, literally 'noble', 'illustrious' (giving the Muslim religious title of 'sharif'), itself the name of an Arabic gold coin. See also **ashrafi** and compare **seraph**. (Portuguese 'x' is pronounced similar to English 'sh', so that the equivalent word for 'shilling', for example, is *xelim*.) See also **bastiao**.

yang
A silver coin of Korea current from 1894 to 1905, when
the currency was reformed and it was superseded by the
won. The name is the same as that of the **yen**, so means
'round', 'coin'. See also **yuan**.

yefimok
The Russian name of the **thaler** in the 16th and 17th
centuries, when this denomination was imported into
Russia in considerable quantities. Many of them were
overstruck or countermarked in an attempt to create a
distinctive Russian coin that could be used for a high-
value silver denomination (the first were issued in 1654),
so were thus a forerunner of the **rouble** and indeed bore
this word on them. Yefimoks were in circulation only for
about five years, however, and the attempt to create an
original coinage failed because of the considerable
disparity in weight when compared to existing currency.
The name is a Russian adaptation of the original name of
the thaler (or **dollar**) itself, so comes from **joachimstaler**.
Interestingly, the western coin names derived from this
(**thaler**, **dollar**, **daalder** and so on) are formed from the
second half of the name, while the Russian yefimok comes
from the first half (the saint's name, significantly enough
for a country that has long honoured her own saints).

yen (plural, same)
The familiar name of the sole Japanese monetary unit
and coin, introduced as a gold piece in 1870 (equal to 100
silver **sen**), with the silver yen on a par with the United
States **dollar**. Since 1955 the 1-yen coin has been minted
in aluminium. The name is a Japanese borrowing of
Chinese *yüan*, 'something round', 'circle', 'coin', and is
thus exactly the same as that of the Chinese **yuan** itself.

233

yigirmlik (yarimlik, yigirmishlik)
A silver coin of the Turkish (Ottoman) Empire, worth 20 **paras** or half a **piastre**. The various names here relate to this value, so that *yirmi* is 'twenty' and *yarım* is 'half'.

yuan (plural, same)
This is the so-called 'Chinese **dollar**', established as a basic monetary unit and coin of China in 1914 but first struck as a silver dollar-type piece in the 19th century. For centuries before this, the **cash** had been the main Chinese currency unit and coin. The name yuan means 'something round', 'coin', 'dollar', and is thus the same as that of the Japanese **yen** and Korean **yang**. Compare also **won**.

yuzlik
A large silver coin of the Turkish (Ottoman) Empire, equal to 100 **paras** or 2½ **piastres**, and originally intended, when issued in the late 18th century, to correspond to the famous **Maria Theresa thaler**. Its name denotes its value, deriving from Turkish *yüz*, 'hundred'.

Z

zahrah
A copper coin of Mysore, issued in 1792 under Tipu Sahib, Sultan of Mysore, with a value of 20 **cash** and a name that is the Arabic for 'Venus' (literally 'brightness', 'splendour of the east', and also the source of the modern first name Zara).

zaire
The chief monetary unit of Zaire, introduced in 1967 to replace the **franc** (in what was then the Democratic Republic of the Congo) and taking its name from a former native name of the Congo river (which was to become the new name of the republic in 1971). The zaire is equal to 100 **makuta** (see **likuta**) or 10,000 **sengi**.

zecchino
The name of a gold **ducat** of Venice, first struck in the late 14th century and in circulation until the end of the 18th century, when the Venetian Republic was dissolved. The name is truly multilingual, since although it primarily derives from La Zecca, the name of the palace housing the Venetian Mint, this in turn originated in Arabic *sikkah*, 'die for coining' (see **sicca**), and the zecchino itself came to be called **sequin** in France and England, thus coincidentally producing the standard English word 'sequin' for a shiny decorative disc on a dress.

zehner
A 'tenner', and the name of a 10-**kreuzer** or 10-**pfennig** coin. The name has not always been colloquial, and it actually appeared on a series of Prussian pattern (prototype) copper 10-pfennig pieces of 1812.

zlatnik

The name of the first gold coin of Ancient Russia, struck at the end of the 10th century and beginning of the 11th. The zlatnik was similar to the Byzantian **solidus**, and has a name that simply means 'gold' (Old Slavonic *zlato*, modern Russian *zoloto*). Compare the **zloty** and **zolotoy** (below).

zloty

The main monetary unit and coin of Poland, divided into 100 **groszy**. The name, which means 'golden', was originally used of the gold coin introduced in the 16th century as a copy of the Hungarian **goldguldiner**. However, the denomination, despite its literal meaning, has also been used at different times of silver coins, just as the **guldiner** has. It does not therefore follow that all zlotys are or have been gold pieces!

zolotoy

A general name for any gold coin of Russia since the 15th century, especially the **chervonetz**. The name actually featured on some coins, such as the 10-**rouble** piece struck in 1755 under Elizabeth Petrovna, Empress of Russia, which was inscribed (in Cyrillic characters): YELIZAVETIN ZOLOTOY ('Elizabethan golden').

zwanziger

A 'twenty-er', or a 20-**kreuzer** coin, especially the one struck in 1753 in Austria, Hungary and southern Germany in accordance with the Monetary Convention that year.

zweier

A 'two-er', or a general name in the 18th century for any coin with a value of twice a particular denomination, such as a 2-**pfennig** piece of Upper or Lower Saxony, or a 2-**kreuzer** coin of Switzerland.

zwölfer

A 'twelver', otherwise a coin with a value of 12 **kreuzers**, such as the **dreibätzner** of Austria and southern Germany in the 16th century.

236

APPENDICES

The two Appendices that follow are an attempt to present coin names in different related sequences: by origin in Appendix I, and by linguistic sense in Appendix II.

As can easily be seen from a brief look through the entries in the Dictionary, many coin names fall into one or other of a number of categories, relating to their type, origin, size, shape and the like. No attempt to devise a rigid categorisation of the names can easily be made, but the following Appendix I perhaps goes some way towards it. It is loosely based on the categorisation proposed initially by Ernst Stückelberg in *Der Münzsammler* (1919) and modified by Ewald Junge in his *World Coin Encyclopedia* (see Bibliography), although it does not quite accord with the earlier versions, and I have added certain categories that neither previous writer distinguished.

On the whole, the examples of coin names in Appendix I are selective, especially in the longer lists, and I have not included the many compound names such as those ending in '-thaler'.

Inevitably, some names cannot be neatly pigeon-holed in a single category, and a few names thus occur in more than one list. There will be a similar 'cross-fertilisation' between many of the names in Appendix I and those in Appendix II, and in the more obvious cases of duplication, a specific reference will be given at the end of the relevant list.

It seemed best to think of the categories in Appendix II more as 'families' than precise classifications, since the names in each list are linguistically related and interconnected. All is not quite straightforward, however, since it does not follow that all names of the **denier** type derived from the Roman **denarius**, and one would have to look closely at the history of all the coins named **double** to see which of them came first. It similarly does not follow that that first coin was the prototype for all the others, and the list simply shows some extent of the range of 'double' names in different languages. Even so it is certainly true that such names as **crown**, **cent** and **dollar** did indeed serve as models for subsequent issues. It will be noted in some instances that a derivative name is simply a 'copy' of an earlier name rather than a definite translation: examples are the **tala**, **sene** and **kurus**.

The diminutive endings on some derivate names should not go unnoticed, so that **escudillo** really means 'little **escudo**', **vierling** means 'little **vierer**', and **doppelchen** means 'little **double**'. On the other hand, the Italian ending '-one' (as in **grossone**) is an augmentative, denoting a 'big **grosso**'. Diminutives predominate, however, serving either to denote a small coin or simply to act as a kind of affectionate nickname (like the 'little **sixpence**' of the English nursery rhyme, or even the **quidlet**, for an admittedly much larger value).

APPENDIX I
COIN NAME CATEGORIES

1. *Ruler*. Names derived from the ruler under whom a coin was issued, and whose portrait usually appears on the obverse: **abbassi, albertus, alfonsino, amani, antoninianus, barberini, camillino, carlin, carolin, carolus, christinchen, christiner, clementi, collot, daric, enrique, filiberto, filippo, filippone, francescone, franciscus, george, giulio, gregorina, gregorio, jacobus, joao, louis, mahbubia, maravedi, marcello, mocenigo, pahlevi, philip, roverino, sisto, trono, victoria**.

2. *Historic figure*. Names derived from some historic figure regarded as important in the development of a country, such as a patriot, rebel, liberator and the like or an early revered ruler such as one of the imams in the Indian state of Mysore: **abidi, asmani, bakiri, balboa, bolivar, bolivares, colon, cordoba, faruk, haidari, imami, jafari, kazmi, lek, lempira, marti, siddiki, sucre**.

3. *Portrait*. Names deriving more from a portrait than from the person portrayed especially when this is not a current ruler or historic figure. Many such portraits are those of saints, who in some instances, however, do have the same name as the contemporary ruler (often a pope): **ambrosino, angel, angelot, anselmino, apollina, barbarina, bastiao, george, giorgino, giovannino, giustina, madonnina, magdalon, paolino, paolo, patrick, quirino**.

4. *Title*. Names based on a royal or noble title, in whatever language: **ashrafi, augustus, ban, bargellino, imperial, pardao, real, rial, riyal, royalin, ryal, shahi, souverain, sovereign**. See also List 1 (**crown**) in Appendix II.

5. *Mintmaster*. Names based on a particular mintmaster, mint owner, moneyer or the like, who was in some way directly or indirectly responsible for the issue of a particular coin:

atchison, aubonne, bawbee, bodle, boratinki, conant, crimbal, harrington, joey, masson, tympf.

6. *Nationality*. Names derived from the country or people or geographical area where the coin was issued, where it circulated, or for where it was intended. In one case here the coin (**guinea**) was named from the country that provided its metal. This list includes 'major' places, not local ones such as towns and mints (for which see List 7, below): **afghani, argentino, belga, bezant, böhmen, brabant, carantano, colombiano, dauphin, dominicano, grenadino, guinea, indio, lari, lat, ligurino, litas, lushburg, mungu, naira, portuguez, rand, somalo, trento, ungaro, vatu, zaire.**

7. *Local name*. Names derived from a particular town or mint where a coin was first struck or where it first circulated: **anconitano, apuliensis, berner, blesensis, bolognino, brummer, ceitil, florin, genevoise, genovino, gosler, heller, liegnitzer, schnieber, thaler.** See also List 2 (**dollar**) in Appendix II.

8. *Inscription*. Names derived from one word (less often, two) of an inscription on a coin, usually a Latin one: **agnus dei, decus, ducat, fert, franc, gloriam regni, grazia, justo, nonsunt, publica.**

9. *Feature*. Names based on a particular feature appearing on the coin, such as a religious or heraldic device, an animal, a flower, a garment or prominent part of a portrayed figure (such as a beard or hair), or a national emblem of some kind. This is one of the most popular categories there is: **agnel, alicorno, armelino, azzalino, banderuola, barbarin, barbone, batz, bauschen, bigatus, bissolo, bissona, bragone, briquet, cagnolo, capellone, carravino, cavalier, cavallo, cavallotto, colonnato, condor, copkini, diamante, eagle, esphera, florette, gigliato, girasoli, griffon, harp, hatpiece, heaume, kopeck, lis, lorraine, lovetta, mitre, navicella, pagoda, parruccone, pollard, quetzal, rider, rijder, rosary, rosina, schaf, snaphan, sol, spadino, stäbler, stella, stüber, testone, thebe, unicorn, vlies.** See also Lists 3 ('cross') and 5 (**lion**) in Appendix II.

10. *Value*. Names derived directly from a coin's denomination. This is the most obvious of categories, and the most frequent, so only a selection of such names can be given here. All such names denote a number of some kind, either 'straight' or in relation to another, as its multiple or fraction: **altilik, altmishlik, artilucco, baht, bumia, chetrum, cinco, cincuentino, cinquinho, demy, dime, dizain, douzain, dreier, duarius, dwojak, fünfer, hecte, ikilik, medio, mezzanino, neuner, octavo, poltina, qindar, quinarius, quincussis, sechser, semis, sesino, tientje, tlaco, toman, utuzlik, yuzlik, zehner, zweier**. See also Lists 6 (**mil**), 7 (**cent**), 8 (**denarius**), 9 (**quarter**) and 10 (**double**) in Appendix II.

11. *Colour*. Names derived from the colour of the coin, mostly some shade of white (representing silver), yellow (gold) or brown (copper). For names based on 'gold', 'silver' and 'copper' themselves, see List 12 below ('metals'): **akce, albus, asper, baiocco, blaffert, blanc, blanca, canary, marigold, murajola, witten**.

12. *Metal*. Names indicating the metal from which the coin was minted: **aes, altun, altyn, argenteus, aureus, ber, chalkos, chervonetz, gulden, kobo, moidore, ngultrum, nickel, rupee, srebenik, zlatnik, zloty, zolotoy**.

13. *Size*. Names indicating the relative size of the coin, especially when unusually large or small: **agora, anna, bagattino, becs, bob, broad, cartwheel, cob, dandyprat, doit, koban, lepton, minuto, oban, pezzetta, piccolo, sprat**. See also List 12 (**grosso**) in Appendix II.

14. *Shape*. Names referring to a coin's shape or form, including its degree of thickness or thinness, its type of edge (milled or not), and the like: **angster, bender, blob, bonk, bracteate, chuckram, crocard, crookie, dicken, dump, gourde, karbovanets, plack, plaquette, ringgit, roda, schwaren, slug**.

15. *Derivative*. These are the many names (not all listed here) that are based on the names of other coins. In some cases the coins are direct copies of other coins, whether 'fullsize' or in a reduced form. In others the only connection may be simply in the name as a denomination: **angelet, chelin, dirham, dodkin, ducatone, ducatoon,**

escalin, fals, filler, follaro, forint, franco, gosseler, grivenka, grivennik, grivenny, gyllen, haler, hardhead, joe, kas, livre, markka, mealha, merk, metical, oncia, oncietta, onza, öre, pistareen, poltura, pond, riyal, scellino, sequin, siglos, skilling, stiver, tester, thrymsa, tornese, tornez, tostao, trime, yefimok. See also Lists 2 (dollar), 7 (cent), 8 (denarius), 10 (double), 11 (paisa), 12 (grosso) and 13 (solidus) in Appendix II.

16. *Money*. Names that simply mean 'money', 'currency', 'coin' or the like: caixa, cash, denga, dong, dub, fanam, fisca, lilangeni, maille, nummium, pa'anga, picayune, sceat, sen, styca, tsien, tugrik, yen, yuan. See also List 14 (taka) in Appendix II.

17. *Weight*. Names that originated as that of a weight, and later became that of a coin additionally or instead: grain, grano, libra, likuta, litra, livre, mas, miskal, peseta, peso, pound, semuncia, shekel, tael, talent.

These are the largest and most distinctive categories. There are also several smaller ones, such as names based on the *sound* of a coin (clinckaert, pengö, possibly penny), the *quality* of its metal (excelente, hyperper, noble), or the actual method of *minting* or striking (aparas, bit, engenhoso, stampee, stooter). A few Muslim coins have *astronomical* names (akhtar, bahram, kutb, mushtari, zahrah), while other coins have a name that commemorates some historic or religious *event*, not necessarily depicted on the coin (annunciata, battezone, morengo, salute). Finally, some coins have a name that means 'part', 'portion' (bu, ichebu, para, peça, ryo, shu), thus close in category to List 10 ('value').

APPENDIX II
COIN 'FAMILIES'

1. **crown** : names based on some form of 'crown' or Latin *corona*: **coroa, corona, coronato, coronillo, couronne, korona, koruna, krona, krone, kroon.**

2. **dollar** : names related to 'dollar', itself based on **thaler**: **daalder, dala, dalar, daldre, daler, tala, talari, tallero.**

3. **'cross'** : names based on the word for 'cross': **cruzado, cruzeiro, kreuzer.**

4. **'shield'** : names based on the word for 'shield': **écu, escudillo, escudo, scudino, scudo.**

5. **lion** : names based on the word for 'lion': **leeuw, leone, leopard, leu, lev.**

6. **mil** : names based on the word for 'thousand', especially Latin *mille*: **milesimo, miliarensis, mill, millieme, millime, milreis.**

7. **cent** : names based on the word for 'hundred', especially Latin *centum*: **centavo, centenionalis, centesimo, centime, centimo, qindar, santims, sene, seniti.**

8. **denarius** : names based on the Roman denarius or the French **denier**, with a root sense 'ten' (Latin *decem*): **decenario, decime, decimo, decussis. denarino, denaro, dinar, dinero, dinheiro.**

9. **quarter** : names based on a word for 'four', especially Latin *quattuor*. Since the words for 'four' are usually mutually related in different languages (French *quatre*, Spanish *cuatro*, Italian *quattro*, Russian *chetyre*, German *vier*, English *four* itself, etc.), all the following names can be said to belong to the great 'foursome family' (although more frequently as a fraction than a multiple): **chetvertak, chetvertina, cuarenta, cuartilla, cuartillo,**

243

cuartino, cuarto, cuatro, farthing, ferding, fyrk, kwartnik, ort, örtgen, örtli, quadrans, quadrupla, quart, quartarolo, quartens, quartillo, quartinho, quarto, quattie, quattrino, vierer, vierling.

10. **double** : names based on a word meaning 'double', i.e. twice a particular denomination: **dobla, doblado, doblone, dobra, doppelchen, doppia, doppietta, doubloon, duplone**.

11. **paisa** : names based on 'paisa', itself meaning 'quarter': **baiza, besa, biche, naya paisa, pice, pie, poisha, pya**.

12. **grosso** : names based on Latin *grossus* or some derivative, meaning 'big': **gersh, ghurush, groat, groot, gros, groschen, gröschlein, grossetto, grossone, grosz, groten, kurus, qursh**.

13. **solidus** : names based on the Roman solidus ('solid') or some derivative: (?) **shilling, sol, soldino, soldo, sou, sueldo**.

14. **taka** : names based on some form of taka ('coin'): **kyat, tanga, tangka, tankah**.

These are the largest or most important 'families' of related names. Among others are the **penny** ones (**fenig, penni, pfennig**), the 'three' ones (**dreier, dreiling, drittel**), and the **royal** ones as also included in List 4, Appendix I (**real, rial, riyal, royalin, ryal**).

APPENDIX III
CURRENCY ABBREVIATIONS

For most of the currencies of the world an agreed abbreviation or symbol exists, usually placed before a numerical sum to indicate a particular amount, such as the well known '£500' to indicate 'five hundred pounds sterling' or '$6000' to mean 'six thousand dollars'. Below are given the commonly found abbreviations for many of the modern currencies featuring in the Dictionary. For convenience, the list is divided into two, with the first half giving the abbreviations that consist of standard letters of the alphabet, and the second containing abbreviations that are really symbols, although often devised from actual letters. (See respectively **libra** and **dollar** in the Dictionary for the origin of the two best known currency symbols, '£' and '$'. The latter appears below as if 'S' alphabetically, even though not deriving from this letter.)

The second half of the Appendix also contains abbreviations that consist of a combined symbol and letter(s).

As with the coin names themselves, there is frequently a variance of usage, with some currencies known by more than one abbreviation. The Dutch gulden (or guilder or florin), for example, can be indicated by 'F' or 'Fl' or 'G', and many African countries use either 'F' or 'Fr' for 'franc'. This explains why some currencies appear more than once in the lists below.

It can be assumed that the given abbreviation relates to all modern countries where the particular currency prevails (see the Dictionary entries under the name concerned). However, where an abbreviation applies to a common currency name in one country exclusively, the country will be stated. It goes without saying that there are many countries besides Britain, the United States and France, for example, where the main currency is known respectively as the pound, the dollar, or the franc.

It will be noted that the dollar sign is the most versatile, since it represents more than one currency. This is because of its basic Spanish origin (see the coin name in the Dictionary).

A: LETTER ABBREVIATIONS

Af	afghani
B	baht, balboa, bolivar
BD	dinar (Bahrain)
CS	cordoba
D	dalasi, dinar (Tunisia), dong
DA	dinar (Algeria)
DH	dirham (Morocco)
Din	dinar (Yugoslavia)
DjFr	franc (Djibouti)
DM	deutschmark (compare OM, below)
Dnr	dinar (Yugoslavia)
Dr	drachma
EB	birr (see also list B, below)
Esc	escudo
F	florin (i.e. gulden), florint, franc
FBu	franc (Burundi)
Fl	florin (i.e. gulden)
FMG	franc (Madagascar)
Fr	franc
G	gourde, guarani, gulden (i.e. florin or guilder)
Gld	gulden (i.e. florin or guilder)
GS	syli
ID	dinar (Iraq)
JD	dinar (Jordan)
K	kwacha, kyat
Kčs	koruna
KD	dinar (Kuwait)
Kr	krona, krone
L	lek, lempira, leu, lira
LD	dinar (Libya)
Le	leone
Lit	lira (Italy)
Lt	lira (Turkey)

Lv	lev
M	mark
MF	franc (Mali)
Mk	markka
N	ngultrum
OM	ostmark (i.e. East German mark)
P	pataca, peso (Colombia, Philippines)
P (plural, Pts)	peseta
Pt	punt (after 1979) (see also list B, below)
Pta	peseta
Q	quetzal
QDR	riyal (Qatar)
R	rand, rial (Iran), riyal, rouble
Rd	rand
Re (plural, Rs)	rupee
RO	rial (Oman)
S	schilling
Sch	schilling
SFr	franc (Switzerland)
Sh	shilling
Tk	taka
Tug	tugrik
UD	dirham (United Arab Emirates)
W	won
Y	yen (see also list B, below)
Z	zaire
Zl	zloty

B: SYMBOL ABBREVIATIONS (with or without conventional letters)

¢	cedi, colon
£	pound, punt (before 1979) (see also list A, above)
£E	pound (Egypt)
Fl£	pound (Falkland Islands)
Gib£	pound (Gibraltar)
L£	pound (Lebanon)
£SY	dinar (Southern Yemen)
£T	pound (Turkey)
₦	naira
$	dollar, escudo (Portugal), peso, ringgit
$A	dollar (Australia, Kiribati, Nauru)

B$	dollar (Bahamas, Brunei)
$B	peso (Bolivia)
Bds$	dollar (Barbados)
Cr$	cruzeiro
E$	birr (see also List A, above)
$F	dollar (Fiji)
G$	dollar (Guyana)
HK$	dollar (Hong Kong)
J$	dollar (Jamaica)
NZ$	dollar (New Zealand)
RD$	peso (Dominican Republic)
S$	dollar (Singapore)
TT$	dollar (Trinidad and Tobago)
WS$	tala
Z$	dollar (Zimbabwe)
￥	yen
៛	riel

SELECT BIBLIOGRAPHY

A vast number of books have been and continue to be published on the subject of coins – one estimate mentions a possible fifty new publications per *month* – so any type of select bibliography here must be very select indeed. The dozen and a half books listed below were, thus, the ones I found the most useful and consulted the most frequently when compiling the present Dictionary.

Apart from these specialist works, I also consistently consulted standard English (and occasionally foreign) dictionaries such as the *Oxford English Dictionary* and *Webster's Third New International Dictionary* for the etymologies of coin names, where they could be obtained. The *OED*'s inclusion of foreign coin names is somewhat uneven and unpredictable (in the *Supplement*, the basic principle seems to be that the coins of former colonial countries are likely to be included, while others are not), and on the whole *Webster* has the slight edge when it comes to comprehensiveness and etymology. Many smaller modern dictionaries are unwilling to give the meaning of non-English coin names, even though they will often indicate the language of origin. This is not enough, however, for the present Dictionary, since the original meanings of the names is precisely what it aims to reveal. On the whole, therefore I did not have much occasion to resort to contemporary single-volume dictionaries, admirable though they may be in all other respects.

If I had to name a really select selection of useful works for coin name meanings and origins, I would recommend those by Fengler, Gierow and Unger (for the reader who knows German or Russian), Frey, and Schrötter (again, in German). These three works have their particulars included below.

249

Carson, R.A.G., *Coins*, Hutchinson, London, 1962.

Chamberlain, C.C., *The World of Coins: A Dictionary of Numismatics*, revised by Arthur Blair, Hodder & Stoughton, London, 1976.

Fengler, Heinz, Gierow, Gerhard, Unger, Willy, *Lexikon der Numismatik*, Transpress, Berlin, 1982. (A Russian version of the previous (1976) edition was published in Moscow also in 1982.)

Frey, Albert R., *Dictionary of Numismatic Names*, Barnes & Noble, New York, 1947.

Grierson, Philip, *Numismatics*, Oxford University Press, 1975.

Hazlitt, William Carew, *The Coinage of the European Continent*, Swan Sonnenschein & Co, London, 1893.

Junge, Ewald, *World Coin Encyclopedia*, Barrie & Jenkins, London, 1984.

Krause, Chester L. and Mishler, Clifford, *Standard Catalog of World Coins*, 11th ed., Krause Publications, Iola, Wis., 1985.

Narbeth, Colin, *The Coin Collector's Encyclopaedia*, Stanley Paul, London, 1968.

Rawlings, Gertrude B., *Ancient, Medieval, Modern Coins and How to Know Them*, Ammon Press, Chicago, Ill., 1966.

Schön, Günter, *World Coin Catalogue: Twentieth Century*, 4th ed., Barrie & Jenkins, London, 1982.

Schrötter, Friedrich von, *Wörterbuch der Münzkunde*, Berlin-Leipzig, 1930.

Sédillot, R., *Toutes les monnaies du monde*, Paris, 1955.

Yeoman, R.S., *A Catalog of Modern Coins*, Western Publishing Co., Racine, Wis., 1978.

Zvarich, V.V., *Numizmaticheskiy slovar'*, 4th ed., Vishcha shkola, L'vov, 1980.